JUNGIAN BIRTH CHARTS

An explanation of how the four element
in astrology relate to Jung's four types —
thinking, feeling, sensation and
intuition.

JUNGIAN BIRTH CHARTS

CHARTS

How to interpret the horoscope using Jungian psychology

Arthur Dione

THE AQUARIAN PRESS
Wellingborough, Northamptonshire

First published 1988

© ARTHUR DIONE 1988

British Library Cataloguing in Publication Data

Dione, Arthur
Jungian birth charts: how to interpret the
horoscope using Jungian psychology.
1. Astrology and psychology   2. Psychoanalysis
I. Title
133.5'01'9   BP1729.P8

ISBN 0-85030-642-6

*The Aquarian Press is part of the
Thorsons Publishing Group,
Wellingborough, Northamptonshire, NN8 2RQ, England*

Printed in Great Britain by
Woolnough Bookbinding Limited,
Irthlingborough, Northamptonshire

1 3 5 7 9 10 8 6 4 2

CONTENTS

Dedicated to my colleagues at the B.A.S.

FOREWORD

This book is intended not only for those with a little astrological knowledge and who wish to explore the deeper realms of the individual chart, but hopefully also for a general audience, since it explores more than one theme. Astrological students, it is hoped, will benefit from being able to use Jungian symbols in horoscope interpretation, though it is not intended specifically as a cookbook. The layman may find something of interest too, since it is not specifically a book on astrology—I have tried to embrace as wide a spectrum as possible, calling upon philosophical themes, fairy-tale motifs and down-to-earth commonsense psychology. It attempts to weave the threads of astrological knowledge into those of Jungian symbolism (or is it the other way round?) in order to clothe the reader with an enhanced knowledge of psychology and the horoscopic art.

Astrology is about daily living, here and now, in the twentieth century, and we are in for a fairly long wait before the people who reject the subject out of hand open their eyes and ears and allow their stiffened egos to lower the barrier and simply 'listen'. The ones who have already decided that it doesn't 'work' are the ones who refuse to look beyond their noses to what is happening in and around them, the situations for which they are responsible, the people they attract and the messes they create through continually blaming others.

All of the myriad forms that life constitutes can be found lurking somewhere on the birth chart, under the skin of the individual himself. Both depth psychology and its older sister astrology point to the real selves trying to get out and finally see the light of day.

While this is not actually a book about the work of Carl G. Jung, it pays tribute to the profound depth and insight of the man himself in virtually every chapter, by attempting to bring his subject closer to a general audience already aware of the validity of astrological knowledge.

INTRODUCTION

The ancient art of astrology is still denigrated as a medieval type
of soothsaying even today, due to the popular trend of quack
newspaper horoscopes. It's easy to pick up the morning tabloid over
one's cornflakes and turn to the page where Madame Zelda tells you
that romance is favoured tonight, or that you might find disfavour
with the boss today, but it takes some degree of responsibility to
accept that we ourselves are the ones running the show. Not only
are we the main attractions—we are also the producer, the director
and even the audience. Human beings have a knack of drawing
qualities out of others which are a by-product of themselves; they
are quite simply attracting that which they lack.

Not only do they lack a well-rounded personality but they lack
the insight to see into themselves. This is the beginnings of wisdom,
but we need a starting-point. One point of departure for this gaining
of self-knowledge is astrology. Many competent astrologers have
recently tried, via statistical evidence, to validate the subject in
scientific terms but astrology has never been and never will be a
science. Science concerns itself with the postulation of a theory which
can be demonstrated by way of an experiment; it then catalogues
the results and draws its conclusions as to how the results come about.
Therefore it can demonstrate that A plus B really does equal C.

What then is one to do with this obscure subject? Why—
popularize it, of course. I have attempted in the following chapters
to explain in simple terms the basis of depth psychology and how
it may be used with astrology. Not only is this a workbook using
two interpretative systems at once, it is an introduction for the layman
to the curious, often magical world of the unconscious. The heroic
quest is a theme which repeats itself through countless myths and
fairy-tales and it is this same quest that confronts us in our daily
life. Modern man perpetuates the stories of his daily life, he plays

the part of the hero 'rescuing the damsel in distress and slaying the dragon' and struggles ever onward to gain mastery of himself.

If we appear to be digressing somewhat from depth psychology, remember that these symbolic quests reappear in dreams, as spontaneous products of the human psyche. Often, dreams that involve roads, buses, trains or any familiar form of transport, symbolize one's trials on the journey through life and it is helpful to acquaint oneself with the general, universal meaning of the symbol itself before trying to unravel the whole meaning of the dream. Dreams are the domain of depth psychology and Jung began with the supposition that the dream, however vague or unclear, means to convey something important to the dreamer that the unconscious has 'thrown up' and tried to communicate in its own peculiar language. It is interested in why those results come about in such a way and searches for the most logical reasons for the evidence. Therefore something 'caused it to happen'.

Astrologers, on the other hand, do not concern themselves, as a rule, with *why* human beings behave differently when born under different planetary configurations. They tend simply to accept the correlation of the positions of the planets in the solar system with man's inner nature. Astrology, they argue, has been a recognized phenomenon since the beginning of time; we know that it *does* work, even if we don't know exactly *how* it works.

Depth psychology is perhaps not so well-publicized as astrology, but it has been the subject for specialists since Sigmund Freud and his colleagues set the wheels in motion around the turn of the century. One of those early pioneers did much to shed light on the mechanisms of the psyche and gained a place in medical history as a result. His name was Carl Gustav Jung (1875–1961).

There are many well-read and talented astrologers who have studied Jung. His work is a useful companion to horoscopic interpretation in that the fundamentals are very much the same, only its language is different. Depth psychology and astrology ought to be used in cooperation with one another when looking at charts because it is obvious that they complement one another—which I hope to show in the chapters which follow.

1.
LORDS OF THE UNDERWORLD—
IT'S ALL IN THE MIND

Why do we attempt to predict our futures through consulting horoscopes? Could it be that we are driven by a deep-rooted insecurity to make predictions where 'it will all come right' or 'the dream will finally come true', having our palms read at the seaside, seeking the guidance of the astrological counsellor or sitting before a table strewn with an unusual though colourful, antiquated deck of cards?

How do these seers know anyway? What strange unseen powers lurk behind the velvet drapes on Blackpool's Golden Mile Promenade? Why do so many people need a guarantee on the future in the same way that one can obtain twelve months' free parts and labour on a new automatic washing machine? Is there such a guarantee on life? And if there were one, would we buy it? The fact remains that life for most people is as unpredictable as the people themselves, or as good old British weather. We are all responsible for creating the life around us, using some vague power that we call attraction; 'like attracts like' you may say, but so do opposites, and the latter experience is often a painful encounter.

It all rests squarely on the individual whether or not he will land a new position with the company, get a promotion, get more money, find a lover or travel abroad on sumptuous foreign holidays—because, as in all nature, there is the fact of change and we are as much a part of nature as the grass growing on the front lawn. All of us, like the animal kingdom and the plant kingdom, are limited to a lifespan of so many years, steadily becoming older and older, subject to the same loves and hates, pleasures and pains, joys and tears and irreconcilable pairs of opposites from which it appears there is no escape. The more we search for pleasure, often with hedonistic fervour, the more we are inviting the same experience turned on its head, the experience of pain. This counterbalancing in nature is evident in the findings of depth psychology, astrology and other occult subjects but has its roots in Taoism. This is the Chinese philosophy that says all is created through an interplay of opposites, positive (yang) and negative (yin)—which does not suggest that one must cancel out the other, but rather that they are necessary to each other if there is to be wholeness and completion.

This wholeness is reflected in the birth chart of an individual, containing a number of positive energies, and either a complementary set or imbalance of negative energies showing the inherent predisposition of an individual who can only view life his way. That is, according to the positions of the planetary bodies located against a backdrop of zodiacal signs and houses. He is able only to see what he allows himself to see, that is the way in which he can see best, approaching life through the energies manifested at the time of birth, which is the moment at which he has been summoned to the drama that has been going on since who knows when.

It is as if he had just arrived at the cinema to watch a film that started half an hour ago. On entering the stalls he is aware only of the plot so far, noting the surroundings of the film-set, the performers that he will encounter and the general mood and flavour of the film itself. This can be translated into the general temperament of the individual (plot), the environment to which he is born (film-set), the sum total of experiences in relationships (other performers) and the capacity for individual development and growth (mood and flavour of the movie). The plot and the general mood are, of course, interspersed in the movie and one may draw a distinction here between the predisposition of an individual and the general pattern of his life only when he is separate from those experiences.

Herein lies the problem for many of us. Inevitably at some point we will have to stand up, turn around and leave the cinema for good, but during our stay we tend to view the situation around us as being separate, split and diffused, trying to relieve ourselves of thoughts and emotions that are all too obviously part of us. One's general pattern of life, so to speak, is determined by the psychological factors existing in the psyche, or mind. The birth chart is a general layout of one's psyche, full of creative energy needing to be released out into the world, yet we often fail to express that potential in full. Having determined one's intentions and the way in which life is experienced, there is then the problem of balancing the yin and yang.

The search for pleasure leads us to neglect the opposite side of life. Immediately one is fencing oneself off from certain parts of nature, trying to hang on to the other half. We do not want to give up the pursuit of pleasure, for we are only too aware what it is like to be lonely, sad, empty and depressed. So we build up a hundred and one defence mechanisms, anything in fact to spare us the one thing from which we all recoil in horror—psychological pain.

We cling to the pleasant experiences locked in our memories, therefore the past, and want constant reassurance that we will be able to perpetuate this gratification of pleasure throughout days to come. We want a tremendous amount of security, yet nothing that nature ever produced had a static, secure existence, save for lumps of rock and even they are eventually eroded away.

Perhaps all this sounds too depressing, yet underneath these manifestations is a life-force that cannot be changed or altered lest one run the risk of violating nature's laws, and if one is prepared to 'go with the flow' and let go to nature, there is a simple happiness and joy that goes completely beyond the accumulation of pleasure. When nature decides to move, it is better to go along with the very flow of nature itself. When at some point one experiences a painful situation, often indicated (by transit) on the birth chart, how is one to remedy the tangled psychological mess that ensues? Frankly, there is no escape from the present.

The Ego is a Very Lonely Man
The symbols used in depth psychology and astrological delineation vary only in shape; their meanings point to the same inner motivation, to integration, balance and wholeness. The changing nature of the universe is reflected in the birth chart as the planets steadily continue in their orbits around the Sun and symbolically around the horoscope wheel, demonstrating that life is not a static thing. As soon as we appear to have a fixed birth chart, we have to realize that at the same time, the planets are perpetually in motion continuing the journey which they began at the moment of birth, symbolically re-enacting the psychological progress of the native himself. Astrologers call this 'progressions'.

The whole universe that we know may be 'contained' within an imaginary sphere, housing all of the planetary bodies in an apparently random succession of positions. The psyche likewise when laid down in diagram form is best represented, although never definitively, using the analogy of the sphere. Here, for the purposes of explanation and classification, the mind is split into two halves, the conscious and unconscious, and like the yin and yang they are compensatory to one another. Consciousness is becoming aware of a given experience; I am able to say that 'I know' because I have come to realize that *it* is there, whether *it* is psychic or physical. Again we have achieved the split between inner subjective awareness (moods, feelings, memory, hunches) and outer objective awareness (physical sensations) but have you ever tried experiencing the world without a subject? We need a focal point for consciousness, otherwise there would be nothing but chaos stemming from unconscious impressions and affects, therefore there must be something in us managing to make sense of the world via a process of exclusion. The gatekeeper of the conscious mind we have called the ego, often a very lonely man indeed.

The conscious mind holds to itself everything that is dear: sweet, pleasing memories, gentle feelings, belief, conviction, knowledge—and proudly holds a mirror to itself, reflecting the thoughts corresponding to its self-image. This focal point in the conscious mind is to achieve distinction from elements in the psyche of which one wishes to remain unaware. The mind 'sees' only what it wants to see, demonstrating that ignorance really can be bliss. If the ego cannot acknowledge the presence of a particular feeling about something, it tries everything in its power to banish it—relegating it to the unconscious, though failing to diminish its power. Take for instance the feeling of guilt: the ego will assign itself the power to eliminate the thought, lest it have to admit to it, and for a while may succeed in forgetting what at this particular moment is an uneasy, nagging sense of conscience or self-doubt. The ego raises its knuckled finger and the mind moves on to other things, anything, just to forget the present feeling. But during this process, the ego has also noticed the reason for the state it finds itself in at the moment; it is in a defensive mood because it had to resist 'something' or other, so instead of acknowledging those feelings it has to ignore their very existence. The ego simply loves being in the right. So all the time, it has recognized that the reason it is moving away from its original thought is to forget that it is feeling guilty. No wonder we screw our minds up and blame others for our inability to cope with the truth.

We are afraid to admit our weaknesses and when the ego develops lopsidedly, that is, seeking to become aware only of what it deems suitable, human beings see only what they wish to see. The ego is indeed a lonely man, one whose function is to regulate the attentions of the conscious mind and draw the curtains on anything that one wishes to exclude from everyday consciousness. It is a gatekeeper, admitting only those who qualify to be recognized in the sunny gardens of the upper levels; meanwhile, there is a gravedigger working in confrontation with the man on the gates. He rules the underground that is in direct proportion in weight and size to the emotional experiences and sensations of the conscious mind. The person who owns this garden has filled it with all sorts of pleasant-smelling, colourful flowers, plants and trees. There is a small shed where he keeps his possessions, and not surprisingly he is extremely proud of them. What a fine piece of landscape it is, a few rough spots perhaps but they can easily be weeded out with a little effort. Underneath this protective face of landscape are the nether regions, the discarded elements of personality. It would be unsuitable to describe this zone as the repository for repressed, unusable content, for the unconscious often comes to our aid in times of greatest need.

The above analogy of the 'pretty' garden serves to illustrate man's efforts to implant certain qualities into conscious awareness, thus building a self-image with which he feels safe and one that is palatable to his parents, associates, friends and lovers. Any inner urge that is squashed lest one run the risk of reproach from others, does not disappear, but remains down there, underneath that 'lovely garden' which we are pleased to show off. These natural instincts grow and collect qualities of their own, forming a second personality that Jung called the Shadow.

The Secret Life of the Unconscious

The Shadow side of the personality is that natural urge in us towards baser instincts, our darker aspect that we continually hide not only from others but from ourselves. Most of these primitive instincts when obeyed in everyday life are called evil—consider for example the Christian Church's condemnation of the 'sinful pleasures of the flesh'. Let's look at these instincts from a psychological point of view. Just exactly what is to be called evil? Murder, rape, mugging and fraud may be somewhere high on the list of beastly pursuits; crime has continued unabated for thousands of years and people still kill their fellow human beings.

Could it be the work of the devil? Or could it be that there is something evil in each and every one of us, just as there surely must be some good. We are apt to criticize our neighbour's faults when they do not correspond with our image of propriety, but surely this is only a moral question. When the ego has recognized itself and its apparent glamour, it prefers to keep the unacceptable contents hidden, but since these elements have an emotional quality, therefore an energy content, it is as if they have a life all of their own. Remember the transformation from Dr Jekyll to Mr Hyde in R. L. Stevenson's classic?

The shadowy energy seeks expression, like any other element of the unconscious that is denied entry into the individual's 'pretty garden' above the surface. This is the secret life of the unconscious and the term used when unconscious elements 'find their way out' into consciousness—through others—is called projection. One hears talk of 'projection of an image' and this is half of the mechanism that occurs. Jung has said that everything unconscious is projected, which therefore does not simply mean the qualities that we have disowned due to their unacceptability.

The contents of projection are backed by an 'energy' that makes them more than a mere image. An image imbued with energy takes on a life of its own and our unconscious sides are mirrored in a suitable object who in some way represents those qualities. These qualities are factors in ourselves, of which we were entirely unconscious, but have been mirrored in the object and made visible. We are drawn to that which we lack, due to the natural pull of opposites and we lack the recognition of our faults and inadequacies.

The ego thrives on always 'being right' and assumes control of the life of an individual. We become involved with people who personify the worst in ourselves, the antithesis of our ego identifications. Projections of the Shadow are to those of the same sex as ourselves, and even if we have acknowledged that we are not one hundred per cent perfect, we cannot abide having to contend with our so-called evil side. It is much easier to blame 'them' for our relationship break-ups, bad moods and failures. It is always that mysterious 'they' who are responsible for our being fired from work, jilted in love affairs or not having 'got anywhere' in life.

Where consciousness is lacking, we attract those people who will play the role that we are unconscious of, then we find them either strangely attractive because they are so 'different' or completely repellent because we dare not face our unconscious side. The psyche is merely carrying out its natural 'function' to perpetuate a balance, and any individual unaware of his inner self (subject) receives the compensating other half of his psychic content through attracting others (object) by projection.

The Shadow is an instinctual part of nature, quite close to us, in fact, something to which our primitive ancestors would attest. The animal in man is unleashed when the need for survival is paramount, a fact displayed brilliantly in William Golding's *Lord of the Flies*. Society would frown on such behaviour of course, and we try to adapt ourselves in accordance to what is expected of us by our fellow men. Not every one of us can live up to those expectations and we witness behaviour that is 'out of character' from generally 'normal' types in sudden, violent outbursts and fits of rage. Here, the Shadow bursts forth, spewing the contents into consciousness and invading the ego but providing a much-needed release from the constraints of the environment. The Shadow persists in finding an outlet for its instincts, yet society forbids.

The Shadow is merely one's Achilles heel, but it is painful for an individual to admit his weaknesses, let alone try to permit them into consciousness. The shadowy side of our nature is usually swept under the carpet in the hope that it will not raise its ugly head ever again. But it does, mirrored in the projection of one's unconscious self. The recipient of our undeveloped, somehow stunted qualities seems possessed of all the traits we know ourselves to despise. They are part and parcel of the function that is most lacking within us, and since we have no easy access to this function, it remains for the most part unintegrated, dormant and unrecognized. We dislike these characteristics in our condemned neighbour simply because they are so awkward and difficult to come to terms with in ourselves.

Persona and Anima/Animus

Intense projections occur when there is a strong emotional reaction somewhere in the unconscious, living energy that intrudes into the safe, secure kind of consciousness. As shadow projection occurs and we blame others for our imperfections, the ego smartly prides itself on cracking the whip in its own home, but as mental patients and severe neurotics will tell you (and I've talked with more than a few of them) the ego is not always king of the castle. Such powerful projections of a different kind come into play when there is an emotional involvement with a member of the opposite sex; this stems from the contrasexual element existent within each human being. Every man has certain so-called 'feminine' qualities, and as they are contrary to his outward appearance, remain once more in the depths of the psyche. The so-called outward appearance is the self-image one fosters in order to function within the framework of society. The face that looks outward must please our fellow human beings to some degree so that we can cooperate, make contact, receive praise and generally propose a suitable mask to the outer world. This mask Jung called the Persona, and it is to all intents and purposes the mask that I show to the world. We cannot feel right about ourselves if we do not present an acceptable face to our friends and colleagues, and the clothes and cosmetics industry have been a safe market ever since the word 'fashion' (taken here in the context of what is 'in fashion' or 'fashionable') appeared on the lips of man.

We even go so far as to buy the right clothes and wear our hair in a certain way because it is the current trend. In dreams, clothes are symbolic of an outer façade and relate directly to Jung's conception of the persona. To dream of being naked (therefore without clothes) suggests the inner desire to be free of all outward pretensions and 'false' behaviour, therefore to 'remove the mask' and reveal one's inner self.

The persona then is the face that looks outward, pointed towards the conscious life, under the guidance of the articulate, though sometimes stubborn ego. The contrasexual figure I mentioned earlier forms another face in the unconscious and does the reverse of what the persona does, namely looks inwards to the unconscious. Jung called this figure the anima in men, and the animus in women. Anima means more or less 'soul-image' and animus corresponds to the idea of 'wind' or 'spirit', the impersonal body that lives within woman, dictating to her the qualities of reason, independence and fighting spirit. Where the feminine soul in the male consists of responses, moods and feelings (suggesting the element of water) the male counterpart of the woman thrives on opinions, assumptions and impersonal thought (suggesting the opposite element of air).

From where, then, do these factors arise? Are we but merely toying with an idea, a concept? The anima and animus are no mere inventions of the glib, articulate conscious mind, they are, like the mind itself, full of living energy. In this sense, they are like little personalities, since anything unconscious tends to become personified, either in dreams or more commonly in projection. Anything with an energy content therefore, comes to life.

What Does the Anima Want?

There are at least two common sources from which the soul-image derives. Being an unconscious entity, it suggests that we are actually born housing this element within ourselves. The human male has a degree of feminity in his physical constitution, even though he generally feels he must at all times display his masculinity. The psychic aspects of feminity, such as subtlety, sensitivity to atmosphere, gentleness and relatedness are often weak in the so-called 'typical' male. Then they become an inferior part of masculine psychology and are relegated to the unconscious, as the properties of the feminine, other-half of him. These qualities are only 'inferior' because they have not been allowed room in his consciousness; his 'feminine' side remains undeveloped, weak and unintegrated. More often than not he discards the contents and lets his wife, lover, mistress embody these energies for him instead.

The difficulty which often occurs is that the projected image is not the same as the object itself. The projection can be very powerful, but sooner or later the discrepancies between anima and real women are likely to emerge. Anima and animus are more difficult to integrate and realize than the Shadow since they are even further away from consciousness and obtain their make-up, in part, from the collective unconscious (described in detail later in Chapter 4) whereas the Shadow is wholly individual, belongs to the same sex and resides in the personal unconscious.

In short, the anima seeks expression; if it is not recognized as being part of oneself it colludes with the conscious contents of an actual female (that is, the qualities associated with her natural expression, therefore personal characteristics) and begins to live there. From that moment onwards, there is nobody home, except the man himself.

When man cannot use reason and opinions in his reactions, he falls back on to inherited patterns of behaviour, almost dangerously close to childishness, so that apart from man's actual feminine psychological aspects (although weak in conscious awareness), there is his actual experience of females during a lifetime to consider.

The first experience of the mother leaves its mark on the psyche of a child, then there are sisters and childhood friends that are liable to receive the projection of the soul-image. These experiences are apt enough to convince the growing male that 'this is the way women are'. He tacitly assumes that women behave in such a way, according to the expectations and demands of the anima. Encountering females that in no way measure up to his unconscious assumptions of 'the way of women', he merely turns off, and this is not simply referring to the physical appearance.

Falling in Love Again—What Am I to Do?

Falling in love at first sight, you may argue, inevitably stems from the attraction to the other's physical appearance, then the mind, then the soul and before long you find yourself in raptures about the person for whom you have waited so long, the divine, spiritual longing for that one, true soul-mate.

Psychologically speaking, the state of in-loveness is due to a mutual agreement between the man's anima and the woman's animus, and while the partners remain blissfully unaware of each other's real, conscious selves, the soul-partners will continue to direct the show. Having said that, this type of experience is psychologically very healthy, if it promotes true understanding, when the projections have worn down and the intensity has diminished. If each partner comes to realize his or her individuality as well as the partner's, whilst maintaining involvement in the relationship, then one has the ingredients for a happy partnership. It is not quite as simple as 'give and take' for individual needs must be met and if they are not, then the unconscious will intervene to 'protect' the contents of the psyche and a splitting off from the relationship may be inevitable.

The theme of transformation at work in fairy-tales suitably illustrates the projection of anima/animus when they find expression in an appropriate object, that of a member of the opposite sex. The only other object seems to be in dreams, where one's unconscious is personified and represented by an actual person (usually known to one) which are really personifications of one's inner, contrasexual qualities.

The anima projection can be perceived in the tale of Sleeping Beauty. Here, the central figure pricks herself on a spindle (a euphemism sometimes for the male principle) and is transported into a state of sleep, therefore unconsciousness, until the moment when the prince comes to awaken her and restore life. Here, it is the male prince's anima that has been brought to life, animating his whole being with a wondrous joy, even the world itself seems a happier place, the landscape suddenly full of brightness once more. As Sleeping Beauty awakes, the whole surrounding forest comes alive once more and is filled with birdsong and light. All is wonder and happiness—just like falling in love!

The animus is less well represented in the various themes of transformation because the unconscious half of the female is relatively impersonal, whereas the anima consists of relatedness and feelings. Yet it has a life of its own, projected onto the male who seems possessed of the qualities of the animus, first having been derived from the father, brothers, friends and so on.

The tale of Beauty and the Beast describes the transformation of a young maiden into womanhood, which can only be achieved through cooperation with the animus. Here there are two animus figures; the first one is the father, who seemingly puts his daughter's life in danger through stealing a rose from the Beast's garden. The garden illustrates the undifferentiated unconsciousness and plucking the rose only suggests 'meddling', but in fact the animus here is attempting to gain access to conscious life, so that the Beast (symbolizing the girl's animus) and the father are the sexual and paternal counterparts of the girl's animus respectively.

By plucking the rose from the garden, an attempt to integrate the animus is made but this is only the beginning of a struggle. The Beast allows the father the rose only if he promises to return with his young daughter Beauty, so that she can live with him (once again, cooperation with the contrasexual figure) in his magnificent palace. Fearful, the father does as he is asked, lest he lose his own life (therefore remain unconscious) and Beauty is eventually installed as permanent guest of the Beast by whom she is quite naturally repulsed and repelled. His dishevelled ugliness is the persona and general appearance of her own animus, not yet awakened into life. Soon though, she learns that her father has developed an illness and begs the Beast to allow her to return and comfort him. (This is a euphemism for a negative aspect of the animus preventing her from attaining the transformation into womanhood, identifying with the father-image and thus remaining psychologically immature.)

The Beast relents and permits her to leave him for one week but declares that he will die without her, so she promises to return when the seven days have elapsed. On arriving home, everything returns to normal for a while until she dreams she sees the Beast dying of a broken heart, desperately awaiting her return. At this, she immediately sets off for the Beasts's palace once again to try to save him, and taking no notice of his ugliness she attempts to resuscitate him. Suddenly she realizes that she has fallen in love with him and that she cannot live without him, even proposing the idea of wedded bliss if he promises not to die. She must save him.

Here is the moment when the ugly beast disappears to reveal a handsome prince, who has been under a spell cast by a wicked witch. When Beauty is able to love the Beast for his own sake, he is granted consciousness and comes to life, revealed as his other face, that of the good-looking prince. Having made this attempt at awareness of her true inner self, Beauty is able to dispense with perpetual childishness (of unconsciousness) and make a real attempt at psychological growth.

This same theme occurs with the release of the anima from the bondage of the mother (which is after all the source from which it derives its influence) when the unsuspecting young hero must first slay a terrible old dragon in order to rescue a young princess, sometimes imprisoned behind the walls of a castle. Often making an appearance is a wicked witch or stepmother who assumes great power over the young maiden and it is this same theme running through the tales of Cinderella and Snow White, that of relinquishing the hold of the possessive mother-figure in order to achieve union with the 'damsel in distress'. It is basically the same prince (masculine consciousness) who needs to undergo various trials in order to 'rescue' the same princess (anima). The implication of rescue exists because the inner soul-figure seeks to be released into conscious awareness and this is only fully realized by some effort on the part of the individual.

2.
WHICH TYPE ARE YOU?
THE ELEMENTS IN ASTROLOGY

How many times have you played the game of trying to guess a stranger's Sun sign by his outward mannerisms and turns of phrase? Perhaps, knowing a little astrology you realize that you may be looking at his Ascendant instead. How many of you rely more on which element is being displayed? Ever guessed that your subject was Sun Capricorn only to discover he was Sun Virgo? Well it doesn't really matter; you would have been half right.

This game is an attempt to classify human beings under certain headings, namely those of the twelve zodiac signs. Virgo and Capricorn are, together with Taurus, capable, practical earth signs. Certain qualities are recognized as belonging to particular elements— fire is active, restless and outgoing; earth is solid, fertile and stands still; air is light, refreshing and moves sideways, managing to avoid confrontation with objects; water is passive, sustaining and seems to blend with whatever object is given to it. Water yields.

It does not need a great deal of intelligence to realize that we are talking about the characteristics of the signs themselves, having been born out of a particular element. Likewise, we say that someone is fiery in order to denote a highly energetic, erratic temperament. The down-to-earth person is simplistic (not to be confused with 'simple') and pragmatic. The airy type is 'breezy' and has the 'light touch'. There are so many deprecatory terms for a so-called 'watery' individual that we need not go into them here, 'wet' being merely one of them. Still waters run deep with this type and the depth of feelings can only be guessed at.

Such classifications are helpful to understand why one person sees things completely differently from another. Human beings are often aghast to discover that their neighbour thinks in an entirely different way. If the effect is not merely one of surprise, it is often that which produces moral offence or an assault on the ego. Arguments and bickerings occur when one disagrees with the other about a subject which may be purely a matter of opinion. Everyone thinks he knows best and because 'I' think it is so, then 'I' have the right to assume everyone else must also. Even when we do not tacitly assume that everyone shares the same opinion or likes the same things as we do, we often find it difficult to 'get on' with those individuals who appear different from us as chalk and cheese. Then why do we attract them?

Jung's Four Types
In *Psychological Types* (1921) Carl Jung studied the problem of typology in detail and proposed four fundamental functions of consciousness from which behaviour is derived. When that function is paramount and subject to continual development by the ego, we have a particular type of function. A strongly Scorpionic person maintains certain qualities throughout life which never leave him, being a natural part of consciousness. If he can be classified as a 'feeling' type, then feeling becomes the superior function. Observe the diagram below:

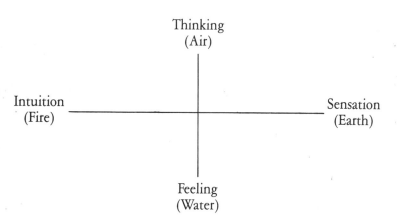

All at once, it may appear that the four psychological types have reduced human beings to a mere classification theory in the same way that—as the layman complains—there are only 'twelve types of human beings in astrology', but in fact, the scope is as unlimited as ever.

Everyday consciousness relies on sense perceptions that merely tell us that something 'is'. An apperception is a process of relating these perceptions to the images stored in our memories of previous experiences, then we are able to identify the experience, whether it is of the subject or the object. These 'functions of consciousness' seem to have been appointed to each individual, everyone possessing a variation on one of them. In order to define each function, let's take a subjective example. But before we begin 'typing', what can we say about the core of each function?

At this core, we discover the polarity of extroversion and introversion. An extroverted type seems happily outgoing, always 'on the move' and devoid of inner motive. He is, in psychological parlance, oriented by objective data, that is, motivated by whatever comes to him from the outside. He often tries to 'fit in' with the group, as if it were more important than him. His consciousness is directed towards the surrounding environment: 'How do I relate myself to the outside world?' is the question on the lips of an extrovert. Whereas, 'how does the outside world fit in with my own life?' represents the general tongue of introverted consciousness. The introvert relies on inner, subjective values as determinants of intention. He is primarily concerned with the personal level of experience and whether or not the group 'fits in' with his own needs and tastes. He is at his best in close communion with others and shuns experiences that may threaten his very personal, rich inner life. The extrovert usually has no such majestic inner world so that the outside world (the environment, community, media, etc.) constantly makes its presence felt.

Extroverted Attitude	*Introverted Attitude*
'How should I relate myself to the rest of the group?'	'What does the group mean to me?'
'Most bachelors over 40 will never marry'	'It depends on the individual'
'I ought to make an effort when the in-laws arrive'	'If I'm not in, they miss me'
'Television can often spoil the art of conversation'	'It depends what you're watching'

It is not my intention to mislead the reader into thinking that introverted consciousness equals a selfish, dull, insensitive clod but it may evoke a similar comment from his extroverted counterpart. The introvert relies on the supremacy of human individuality, mirrored in his reply to the extrovert on the subject of male marriage plans in middle age. The extrovert has used empirical data and becomes a general mouthpiece for consensus opinion. Is it really his own opinion, derived from his own analysis? Probably not. The introvert reacts predictably when he points out in only five words that not everyone can be grouped in such a way, since each individual is different. This is a blessing from the introvert in that it respects the individuality of others.

These two attitudes permeate the functions of consciousness, so that they are halved into not just four, but eight types.

Having said that, introversion and extroversion are interchangeable; what does not seem to alternate is the main function itself. One can have introverted and extroverted thinking, but never a crossover towards feeling, because that is the so-called 'opposite function', the one that cannot be used simultaneously. For thinking to remain true to its element it must be devoid of the prejudice and emotional bias that feeling brings.

The thinking type's inferior function is feeling, and we shall see why, shortly. The two remaining functions may be used to back up thinking and these are termed auxiliary functions. The following table lists the underlying psychic occurrences and motivations towards its particular type. These are not definitions of character but often the 'power behind the throne' that produces those characteristics.

Cores of Psychological Types

Opposite functions
Thinking v Feeling

Rational — Irrational

Impersonal — Personal

Social — Individual

Lightness — Depth
(As in Air)   (As in Water)

Breadth — Intensity

Comparisons — Wholeness

Air — Water
(Surface)   (Underneath)

Opposite functions
Sensation v Intuition

Rational — Irrational

Material — Psychic

Object — Image

Facts — Expectancy

Details — Possibilities

Structured — Changing

Earth —   Fire
(Preserve)   (Create)

The Thinking and Feeling Types
One's sense perceptions tell us that something quite simply 'is'.

Thinking tells us what it is, by deciding what it is not. Therefore it is a process of exclusion in order to recognize something as it is compared with something else. Feeling is to evaluate as to whether something is pleasant or not. To measure the general 'feel' of either object or experience.

Never before was there such a conspicuous pair of bedfellows as these two magnetically attached elements. Air is anathema to Water in its function in the conscious mind, that of deliberate rationalizing and the performance of logic relating one idea to another. Their responses are often spontaneous, even clever or witty, but there is something impersonal, if not cold about the whole charade. Water responds slowly, if at all, but it is observably warm and tinged with human feelings.

Water either simply 'likes' or 'doesn't like', attesting to the theory that there is no accounting for taste. Air tends to trivialize this and makes comparisons but it must be said that Air does not have such strong likes or dislikes as Water.

In the following scenario, thinking and feeling are discussing the previous night's television viewing. Both have seen exactly the same programmes.

Air: Did you see ——— on TV last night?
Water: Yeah, what a load of ———
Air: What d'you mean? It's even better than the last series!

At this, Water turns off, because if the programme in question did not appeal to him personally, there is no point in continuing the discussion. Water responds beautifully though to anything coloured with human emotion, the more pleasant the better. Water types grasp the whole situation instantly. They are sensitive to the needs of others and their reactions are appropriate to the mood of the moment.

Water: The late film was good though.
Air: Oh it's been on before. Anyway I've read the book.
Water: Especially the dramatic ending, it was a shame for the . . .

Water loves the emotional drama, easily sinking into its feelings, often appearing melancholy or even in a state of depression. It was able to be 'touched' by the heartwarming ending of the film, sharing the emotions of the hero, gripped by the intensity of it all. This is the depth referred to in the 'Types' table, striving for intensity and the human touch whereas Air is at home with the light, impersonal attitude, striving for breadth and range. Air was not able to share in the emotional content of the film, being quite content to see the film as a story portrayed by actors under a studio spotlight. It is this 'distance' that allows Air types to stand back and get a clear view of the situation, not only watching television, but in their personal relationships too. Why get involved in such emotional messes, when with a little positive thinking one can keep a clear head and remain on top of the situation.

The truth is that Air does not have the capacity for intimacy, and compensates for this lack by continually relating through ideas and abstractions, something of which Air is very fond.

An obscure, unrelated subject to the feeling type does not make a single impression whereas Air will shuttle ideas back and forth, adaptably and cleverly. Air is therefore very adept socially and its three signs, Gemini, Libra and Aquarius have a reputation for casual, off-the-cuff conversation. The three Water signs, although understanding feelings and emotions better than the other three elements, can even appear anti-social and unwilling to communicate. There is such a depth to Cancer, Scorpio and Pisces that their feelings are not always easy to put into words. So they remain silent.

The Sensation and Intuitive Types

The elements of earth and fire are, likewise, opposite functions, a strong sensation type therefore has intuition as the inferior function. The one that is difficult and uncomfortable, simply because it is undeveloped, as the superior function gains momentum. Sensation perceives via what it receives in plain black and white, a sort of reality function only concerned with physical, practical, commonsense issues. It loves the world of physical sensation and concrete reality effective in managing the material world, thus actualizing its efforts into a tangible result. Therefore its responses can only be based on practical reason, even though it can be overwhelmed by its sensations. This puts it in sympathy with Air, although lacking the abstractions and spontaneity of Air.

The intuition function is the one concerned with the inherent possibilities in a situation. Intuition perceives something via the unconscious often rapidly and instantly without knowing how the idea got there. It is that creative process originating in the unconscious which is often the mother of a very original, enterprising idea so that Fire reacts quickly and often impatiently, needing to burn up the excessive emotional energy it possesses.

In our second scenario, Sensation and Intuition are both

contemplating taking a holiday abroad—unfortunately for them, together.

Sensation: Well, I've made all the plans and the travel agent opens at ten o'clock tomorrow morning.

Intuition: I can see it now, blazing sun, white beaches, a girl on each arm, wild parties . . .

This is typical of these two; Sensation is less concerned with something that has not already happened than his Intuitive friend. Intuition perceives through pictures and has no trouble imagining itself in such a positive light. His faith in himself and the future casts him in an unrealistic light where Sensation is concerned, who wants to stick with the facts and the details.

Referring to the 'Types' table, you will see the words 'material', 'object', 'facts' and 'structured' that are respectively opposed to 'psychic', 'image', 'expectancy' and 'changing'. Our Sensation friend is bound to the world of 'matters of fact'—that is objective, commonsense reality, and he structures his world accordingly. Intuition threatens that secure world with his fondness for creating new experiences, change and usually 'expecting the best'. To Sensation's horror, this is usually exactly what Intuition gets. The 'expectancy' of Fire is a built-in unconscious function which ought to be called 'blind faith', often called 'sickening optimism' by Earth. It is this function that allows those psychic impressions and images of the 'blazing sun' and 'white beaches' to raise the high spirits of the Intuitive. He simply expects to be lucky:

Intuition: I wonder if we'll find that treasure they've been looking for there.

Sensation: Don't be stupid, they haven't found it in four hundred years. Anyway, where's your deposit money?

It is typical of Earth to emphasize and focus on the details at hand. Fire finds this rather too pedantic, feeling threatened and hemmed in. Earth tends to regard Fire as erratic, petulant and impractical. The three Fire signs, Aries, Leo and Sagittarius are visionaries, they have the gift of 'seeing' life's opportunities, then rush in 'where angels fear to tread'. The Earth signs, Taurus, Virgo and Capricorn are representatives of the sphere of materialism, life speaks to them in terms of the physical world, often clever both at acquiring and amassing money. But they would not take half the risks of the Fire signs.

3.
A CIRCLE OF ANIMALS—THE ZODIAC

The Greek word *zodiakos* means roughly 'belonging to animals', something which the ancients interpreted as the belt of sky extending 9° either side of the plane of the earth's orbit around the sun. Only Libra, standing at the gate between subjective personal experience and interrelated collective experience, is represented by an inanimate object. The sphere of man's whole experience is presented in symbolic form through the phases of the zodiac, a cycle beginning with the birth (Aries) and ultimately ending in death (Pisces).

Aries
True to its intrinsic nature, Aries is concerned with births, in the metaphorical sense; new beginnings, enterprise and initiating new ideas and schemes, though it is not particularly scheming in the literal sense. Aries is fond of new ventures while the enthusiasm for it lasts, then they can become easily bored trying to maintain interest if the novelty wears off, consistency not being one of their strong points. The sign needs to express the energies it has, quickly and immediately, enjoying action when it is largely pursued for its own sake. One manifestation of this is in games and sports that require expending a lot of physical energy.

On an inner level, Aries is orientated by the intuitive function and this type of consciousness is fully aware of the 'specialness' of individual human beings and cannot refrain from the need to express themselves as completely as possible. When they do so, they tend to dramatize the situation, actively and cheerfully. This stems from Fire's desire to be recognized, although Aries is not so strongly concerned about this as Leo. Aries desires independence and is not particularly interested in what others are up to, but no one must interfere with their own activities, lest they invoke the notorious Arian temper. Losing one's temper is merely another channel for sudden bursts of energy to find a release.

Aries is generally associated with extroversion, the turning of one's energies towards the outer world, so that it has little time for quiet, reflective behaviour and has difficulty with pursuits that require slow, deliberate concentration. It needs to do what it wants to do at the moment it feels like it, another strongly intuitive trait that is concerned with only the present moment, caring little about the past. To the Aries, tomorrow never comes, but that does not mean that it is unconcerned with the future, since its positive attitude of expectancy normally guarantees it a bright tomorrow. Rather, it denotes that Aries engages itself in a positive 'vision' of tomorrow, in its ideal state, as opposed to accumulating detailed facts about what it will do.

The area on the birth chart where Aries is found, the house that has this sign on its cusp, is approached in the same, positive, optimistic fashion. Aries likes to be in charge, as an expression of its independence, so that this is the area where you like to be first, often putting great amounts of energy into the Aries house. With Aries on a cusp you can be impulsive and often reckless, proverbially 'rushing in where angels fear to tread'.

Taurus

Taurus is a splendid example of one of Jung's sensation types, at home with the five physical senses, fond of creature comforts and upholder of all tangible material reality. As the second sign of the zodiac, it provides matter for the restless, impatient Arian energy, through which it can be made manifest, thus symbolizing the perpetuation and preservation of physical reality. It is through this mode of expression that Taurus signals his fondness for security; to secure something means to fix it in a recognizable form or make it safe and inviolable. This is precisely how Taureans try to live their lives, preferring the black and white stark reality to anything vague and therefore intangible, having a developed sense of the here and now. Their love of tangible reality makes them particularly fond of the most popular symbol of material security that ever existed. Not only are they adept at making money, usually from business ventures and speculation, but are easily predisposed to holding on to it, acquiring a reputation not for meanness but possessiveness.

Life speaks to Taurus only in terms of what is practical common sense, but that does not make Taureans dull or uninteresting. Taurus is often a so-called 'jolly fellow' and noticeably more warm and affectionate than Virgo or Capricorn. He is though relatively simplistic in his general attitude towards life, characterized by his motivation towards security and love of nature, and is attuned most strongly to the physical body. As a sensation type he is particularly interested in obtaining the known facts about something before he will act, and when he does so, it is usually deliberate and slow, exuding thoroughness and persistence. One cannot hurry the patient Taurean and it is typical of this sign to avoid the more flighty, ebullient types who suggest to the Taurus that they have somehow lost their way, for Taurus will not move unless there is a definite reason for doing so.

As an Earth sign it is very close to nature. The female Taurean is extremely fertile in the literal sense of the word, although the sign is not particularly noted for its sensitivity or subtlety. The most striking quality is Taurus' often notorious penchant for possessiveness and stubbornness, both of which are interrelated. Taureans are predisposed to engaging in the process of accumulation, whether of material objects, money or people. They tend to regard partners, friends, associates and husbands or wives as possessions. Jealousy often manifests as the fear of losing something that one holds dear to oneself and it is this same fear permeating the Taurean consciousness when they have reason to suspect that they may be in danger of losing one of their valued, prize possessions.

This brings me to the subject of values. With Taurus on a cusp, there are refined, noble values projected on to that particular house, second best is not good enough here. This is the area where you look for security, stability and are prepared to work in order to preserve it. In other words, it 'means' a lot to you.

Gemini

At the third stage of the cycle, Air is given to breathe life into this as yet inanimate object, so that it may acquire the motion necessary to transportation and communication. The Gemini needs to be free, simply to move around, learning and collecting information about the environment, its virtues being that of adaptability to changes and diversions. With the Air sign, man has acquired the power of reason and versatility, demonstrated skilfully by the Gemini managing to talk his way out of an awkward situation with a detached, cool, articulate grace. It is well within Gemini's range to converse for hours on topics about which he really knows very little, managing to appear as well-informed as the next man. When seriously challenged, he will simply change sides.

This adaptable, casual air usually makes him quite popular in social situations; often quick-witted, clever and humorous, he possesses all of the ingredients for conventional popularity. Although the Gemini is bright and well-informed, he lacks the depth needed to develop an understanding of human behaviour. If they can be seen to exist on the surface, then to him, one's characteristics can be taken at face value and he will seldom bother to notice if there is anything deeper, superficiality being his forte. This stems from Gemini's curiosity and the need to learn as many things as possible in a short space of time and since they learn quickly, they don't see the need to waste time and effort concentrating deeply on any one subject.

Jung's thinking type is extensive in this same fashion rather than intensive, grasping the general picture and then moving on to something else. It is the same process of exclusion whereby A + B = C, so that the thinking type can get a logical view of life where everything adds up and maintains continuity, rather like the scientific approach. His neighbour is well aware of Gemini's fine mind, capacity for interesting conversation and tendency to weigh both sides of the argument before committing himself to an opinion. His reactions often appear like lightning, but then, the Gemini needs to release a considerable amount of nervous energy as he proceeds to demonstrate his prowess at mental and verbal athletics. He has all the virtues of Air: charm, wit, spontaneity, youthfulness and vigour; also some of the vices: hypocrisy, shallowness and transparency.

The two opposed attitudes of consciousness, extroversion and introversion in the thinking type are characterized by what one actually does with one's ideas and where they come from. Gemini with introverted thinking is orientated by the subjective factor and tries to relate his own personal equations (often unrealistic ones) to the surrounding conditions and established facts. Nothing impinges upon him from the external world unless it can be related directly to his own thinking bias.

It is natural for Air to want to be free, to be outgoing and to desire movement. Therefore thinking in the extroverted type seems more in keeping with the nature of this element. Whereas introverted thinking tries to make the tail wag the dog, relying on its own mental gymnastics, thinking in the extroverted attitude seems to have got it the correct way around. This type takes account of all the external facts beforehand, neatly investigating the related parts in order to build a rational framework. He probably does not argue unless he is confident of having all of the facts at his disposal, drawing his conclusions after and not before the experiment.

Introverted thinking often tacitly assumes that it has the answer straight away, when it is obvious that there is some learning to be done. Then it leads itself off on a trail of associated ideas and related assumptions that suggests cleverness and insight but this is far from the case if it has completely chosen the wrong track along which to run its ideas. Extroverted thinking's first concern is in finding the right track before the train of thought gathers speed.

When there is Gemini on the cusp of a house there is a light, off-the-cuff attitude to that area of life. It is the house about which you can intellectualize, need freedom to move around and take a casual attitude towards.

Cancer

With the first Water sign we arrive at the fourth stage in the wheel, that of actual birth and the beginnings of human life. In Aries, the energy preceding birth first appeared, in Taurus it became fused with fertile Mother Earth and with Gemini acquired motion, but as yet is not perfectly formed as a living, feeling entity. In Cancer it is aware of its instinctual needs, the prime necessity for nourishment and growth.

The birth of man takes place in Cancer and drawing from the above sources we observe that Cancer is indeed very much in tune with its emotional needs. Cancer is often sentimental about the past, symbolizing the attunement to all that has been supportive to it in its infancy and the years when it was growing from babyhood to adulthood. Cancerians are fond of their own treasure chest of memories and upbringing, and their interest in their own roots attracts them to subjects like history, religion and, especially, genealogy, the tracing of one's ancestors through the family tree.

Since the feeling function is largely considered inferior in modern society, Cancer has acquired the unfortunate reputation of being a weak, over-sentimental, unstable sign. But these qualities only arise in Cancerians who have not learned to channel those feelings or who are inwardly insecure and vulnerable. Cancer needs to have someone to protect, a solid base and most obviously in women, the desire for children to whom they tend to cling and usually don't recognize that they have grown up, even past the age of thirty. Cancer's needs are so fundamental that it is no wonder that Cancerians acquire the tag of sloppiness and pridelessness, as human pride is yet to completely manifest in the next stage of the cycle.

Feeling is quite naturally an introverted and inward-looking function so that the Cancerian with feeling in the introverted attitude (and this is not to suggest that Sun in Cancer is necessarily a feeling type, though this may be emphasized by other Watery factors) lives through emotional contact with the home and family. Introverted feeling is characterized by behaviour that is determined only by how he feels at any given moment, and therefore by the kind of mood he is in. Nothing can shake introverted feeling out of a mood; his orientation is subjective and the external world simply does not matter to him. He sees no reason to compromise, nor even apologize for the way he feels and is liable to cut off others in social situations when his moods get the better of him. He rises to the top of his own feeling scale, experiencing joy, demonstrating passion and aggression, even managing a touch of euphoria now and then, but equally can sink below the usual depths, drowning in sadness, misery and depression. It all depends on what's going on inside of him at the moment.

His extroverted counterpart, on the other hand, depends on what's going on outside of him. Thus he tries to 'feel his way' into the surrounding environment, and this often produces an extremely sociable, appreciative type. (Extroverted feeling seems very much to suggest the adaptability of Libra, although it is an Air sign). Feeling in this way excludes inner values as the prime determinant, so that we often meet a gregarious, open, generous type in the extroverted attitude who seems particularly ready to accommodate others, unselfish and 'hail fellow well met'.

Cancerians' first love is the family. Nothing else can distract them from the needs of those around them, although they can often alienate the ones they love by extreme swings of mood and changing emotions. Like all the Water signs they are extremely sensitive to those around them, and most of their evaluating is performed without the function associated with thinking. Impressions received from outside are swallowed whole so that they often have a sixth sense that simply 'knows' what is happening in the other person; Cancerians gain an overall feeling about the other person that tells them what they are like. It is pure instinct since Cancer is often in touch with the 'waters of life' but needs to create some kind of base for those feelings; it is one's searching for security. The Cancer area on the chart is where one is able to 'feel one's way' instinctively into the things signified by that house. Emotional security, in all of its many aspects, will be an issue where there is Cancer on a house cusp.

Leo

With Leo we come to the fruition of human individuality, the flowering of the outgoing assertive masculine principle that says 'I am'. It is in this sign that man is bathing in the delights of being human and needs to be recognized as such, often trying to draw attention to himself as he permits himself the centre stage. The birth of man that took place in Water (Cancer) becomes raised to the heights of noble kingship in Leo, and unlike Aries, it needs an audience. It is not a sign particularly noted for humility; even the quiet Leo is secretly very proud and intensely egotistical. When this type of Leo does not make a show of himself, he prefers to express his uniqueness via the creative arts, organization or business. This would still allow him a channel to put forward ego energies that ought to be expressed. When this urge is thwarted, he becomes helplessly vain and petulant, demanding the right to be loved and appreciated without actually having done anything.

This is an unfortunate side to Leo, but like Cancer, it stems from one very fundamental need. The Cancerian needs to have security at an emotional level; the Leo needs to have security at an ego level. That is, he needs to establish his identity and express himself adequately on that level, so it is a type of ego-security. If these signs are not fulfilling those needs, then they become observably childish in their behaviour. This basic desire for the recognition of Leo's individuality by others seems to be their most striking feature, whether it is their physical appearance, possessions or something they have created. They like others to notice these things as having something special about them, especially something they have created, whether a song, painting, piece of sculpture or the most near-perfect creation of all, a new-born child. You can hear the lion roar, 'Look what *I've* made!'

Creative pursuits are those pursued for their own sake, that is, ones without a necessary material goal. It is the act of doing them that counts and not the result, which is where Leo gains his often childlike, sunny nature. The Sun shines because it is enjoying itself giving off solar power, allowing others to bask in its light, not because there is any product at the end of it, not because there is something to be achieved by a certain set of actions. This attitude may be noticeable in every Fire sign and the following passage demonstrates the opposing natures of the Fire (intuition) and Earth (sensation) in their attitudes towards not only 'getting things done' but in reflection of the fundamental attitude to life as a whole.

While one is creatively pursuing an idea (intuition) reflecting on its possibilities and potential, there is nothing actually being produced physically (sensation) as a result of one's labour. Similarly, whilst one is engaged in continual production and effort (sensation) there is little room for creativity or spontaneity. The creative act is not born of effort, it is a completely fresh and vital occurrence and as you cannot 'try' to be spontaneous, you cannot 'try' to be creative.

The above is so designed as to reflect one of the main differences between Leo and the following sign Virgo, although it could also emphasize the Sagittarius–Capricorn, Fire–Earth polarity. Wherever Leo is on the birth chart, the house so affected is subject to the same kingly attitude that the Sun-Leo takes towards life. This is the area where you need to shine.

Virgo

At the sixth stage of the cycle, the feminine counterpart needed to complement the masculine energies of Leo is found in the sign of the maiden, Virgo. It is the second Earth sign, but unlike Taurus, Virgo will cooperate and adapt easily to the existing conditions. Not only does it go along with them, it also tries to improve them. All that is fiery and lordly in Leo becomes sublimated into effort in Virgo. It is as if there has been such an excess of the solar principle witnessed in the previous sign that at the next stage, all there is left to do is attend to matters outside of the realm of human expression.

Virgo finds fulfilment in work well done, studiously attending to the minor details that Leo overlooked, analysing and reviewing the situation presented before it until it has grasped every last aspect. Virgo simply loves pointing out the weaknesses in every situation and cannot abide the fact that there is no such thing as perfection. To them, beauty is detail, and they become lost in a maze of facts and figures trying to assemble the component parts after pulling the whole thing to pieces. They are like the woman who wanted to discover the secret of beauty by plucking the petals from a rose, until of course there was no rose left to look at.

This is a dilemma commonly manifest in all of the strong Earthy (indicative of sensation) types. Since Earth relates to objects, then it is reasonable to assume that sensation is at its purest when in the extroverted attitude. Extroverted sensation, like Virgo, is concerned with the ordering pattern of daily living on a very real, earthy level. Leo is concerned with maintaining the ego through self-expression, Virgo's attention is focused on maintaining the physical vehicle and material world through the expression of effort. Again, as in the previous two signs the needs of Virgo are quite simple for it to operate with ease and enjoy life in general. The need is not quite as deep as Cancer's emotional security or Leo's ego-security but to be fulfilled, it must occur on an Earthy material level. The need is to maintain and assist the continuation of matter through co-operation with the working laws of nature. To maintain the physical body is to look after one's health, to keep the system in good working order thus making an attempt to purge various imperfections. To maintain one's material world is to rise early, take a shower and dress properly, turn up for work on time, attend to the matter with precision and care, all within a certain schedule to which one must keep if one is to maintain so-called reality.

There is another side to Virgo, apart from their often humble and servile 'just leave it to me' attitude and it forms a complementary half to the idea of simply maintaining existence. Virgo is an extremely busy and productive type. Virgoans are not necessarily very creative, but they are not called the workhorse of the zodiac for nothing; they are tireless in their efforts to arrive at the finished product, on the one hand maintaining what they have already begun, and on the other beginning new tasks to which they can direct their considerable energy, whether or not there is an end product in sight.

The house with Virgo on its cusp denotes the area where you are critical, always attempting to do better the next time. You work hard at it though.

Libra

With the seventh sign in the zodiac we arrive at the gateway to man's relationship to the social order. The first six signs describe development on a purely personal level from actual birth to perfection in the material, physical world. In Libra man is now acutely aware of self in relation to others. This was hinted at in Virgo, where there was the demand to relate to external necessity, although in the field of materialism and the physical body.

The seventh sign is the one that defines itself through reflection on others, learning about its own individuality in relation to the other and Librans do seem to place great emphasis on personal one-to-one relationships, becoming involved in as many as they can. This does not mean to suggest permissiveness but rather that Libra often has a poor sense of self, feeling incomplete, alone and even subtly manipulating the partner via their usual charm and easy grace, fitting in beautifully with the decorative surroundings.

Libra is an Air sign, therefore one that is socially oriented, often compromising with the consensus opinion although they are fond of debate. This is used to provide a fair judgement on any particular issue, weighing one opinion against the other with cool, diplomatic clarity but the Libran often has trouble deciding for himself and will ask the opinion of the partner before being committed. As a thinking type, Libra has difficulty with the darker undercurrents of human nature and prefers the more superficially pleasing and glamorous aspects of relationships. Librans are especially in tune with the outer image of whatever is appealing to the eye, giving them a kind of refined polish to their outer demeanour.

It is typical of Libra to be in love with love, that is, under the spell of their unconscious projections, but they often hold a trump card. It is seldom that Libra does not get its own way in relationships. Outwardly they can assume the role of the accommodating agreeable partner, catering to the whims of friends and relatives, yet they know exactly what they want and, more importantly, how to get it. Every successful boss knows that he will get the best out of his employees by first getting them on his side. Every successful Libran knows that persuasive charm works much better as a PR device than giving orders. That way they can even allow the other person to think that they are getting something out of it!

As the seventh sign, it shares the polarity with Aries and the above description of the way in which Libra works is the antithesis of the Arian attitude. Aries likes to lead others, to be in charge, and consequently is fond of giving orders, whereas Libra makes use of its Airy nature with coercion and diplomacy and still manages to dominate. The social aptitudes and personable sheen that Libra possesses makes the sign appear to have a wonderfully warm, human quality but in fact one can detect a certain superficiality because although it is fond of relating, it is only concerned with the surface issues and fares better in relationships that are not heavily laden with the dark beast of emotion.

Aries defines its individuality in a simple, assertive manner and is content to go it alone; contrariwise Libra is not so happy defining itself in its own right, gaining its foothold by having something from which it can refer back to. Librans are not pushy in any sense of the word and they counterbalance the Arian desire for immediate results. Libra does not like to rush, lest it run the risk of spoiling the situation. Things are to be worked out peaceably after both sides of the issue have been calmly considered, unobtrusively coming to an agreement on what is to be done. Good manners cost nothing.

With Libra on a house cusp there is a tactful attitude towards the matters of that house. Sometimes it's 'anything for a quiet life' and you'll use discretion, reason and diplomacy when the things of that house become an issue. Here is where you are striving for a balanced attitude.

Scorpio

Scorpio is the next critical stage in the development of man's awareness of self through others. In Libra he encounters others as they are in relation to himself, so that there is a distancing effect as in all socially orientated encounters. Libra is based on the very idea or notion of relating itself and the Libran learns quickly how to present and adapt himself to others with an agreeable face. He therefore has a knowledge of what is required of him in order to cooperate. Scorpio is based on the flow of feeling that creates all manner of mutual entanglements during exchanges between people. Man has thus come to know others on a very personal level and it is this type of experience to which Scorpio directs its energies, attempting to penetrate into the heart of life's situations with intense abandon. The Scorpio desires to know what is going on beneath the surface so that it can perceive its inner, often hidden meaning. Coexistent with this attitude is the attempt to conceal its own inner self behind a mask of indifference, frivolity or ice-coolness. It is consistent in being able to project any image, other than the one representing its true feelings. Everything is felt deeply and hidden from the prying eyes of spectators; only those close to Scorpio will learn of those burning, seething emotions.

Like all Water signs, Scorpio is very sensitive, and enjoys all the emotional drama that was lacking in Libra. Scorpio does not relinquish those feelings easily because they have such a powerful effect upon the individual. Whatever is down there must be dealt with and it is a lifetime's accomplishment for this sign. The balancing effect comes through its opposing element when Scorpio has dealt excessively with its emotions.

When there is intense emotion and such swellings of feeling (Scorpio), the experience becomes top heavy and we start to drown in our own oceans of thought. Then, it is necessary to come up for air (Libra) after a prolonged underwater swim, to refresh oneself in the cool, clear air of reason.

Because Scorpio can experience the heights and depths of emotion, it tends to go to extremes in most things. It can sink to the lowest levels of degradation and human depravity but ascend to the noblest, divine heights of which man is capable. It can be excessively greedy and lustful and is capable of extreme self-denial and spartan behaviour. Scorpio will swing from one pole of experience to its complete opposite when it feels it has tasted too much. Its dilemma lies in how to attain the happy medium when it is Scorpio's birthright to pierce the very heart of something, for only that way can they attain real depth.

Scorpio does not care for Libra's coquettishness and will often remain silent, if it has nothing very profound or appropriate to say. Coupled with its intense emotional nature, it has acquired a reputation for being a dark, sinister, brooding figure among the signs of the zodiac. No other sign knows about the emotional aspect of good and evil as much as Scorpio and they remain the mysterious and secretive characters that they are as long as they continue to hide everything about themselves. Part of this stems from the difficulty in verbalizing such powerful feelings, for words are simply not enough to convey the passion and burning desire that lives through the Scorpio individual.

One trait not often remarked upon (lest the astrologer cause Scorpio acute embarrassment) is his soft-heartedness when it comes to relationships or family. Scorpio will tear himself apart seeing the suffering of those he loves and it is at these moments when the going gets tough, that the tough Scorpio gets going.

Scorpio on the cusp of a house makes you intense, secretive and passionate about the affairs of that house. This house is imbued with will-power, toughness and the attentiveness of a steel-trap mind.

Sagittarius
In this the ninth sign, man leaves behind the sphere of personal encounters, having experienced all there is to experience in Scorpio. In addition to dividing the zodiac in half into personal and relationship issues, the signs can be split into three groups of four, beginning with Aries–Cancer (personal, individual growth), Leo–Scorpio (fulfilment through encounters with people and material issues) and the last segment Sagittarius–Pisces (involvement with broader, social concerns). During the first four signs it may be noted that man is developing awareness of self and a support system, it is only in the next four that he needs the involvement of others, whether to be loved for himself, appreciated for work and service, partnered on an equal basis or merged in mutual feeling with a mate. The Fire sign Sagittarius draws man away from such matters and takes him into the realm of higher learning. Having encountered the partner on a deep one-to-one emotional level in Scorpio, there is so much more to be achieved and that must take him in the opposite direction; whereas Scorpio strived for intensity, Sagittarius looks for breadth and tries to experience just as much, and as often as possible. This attitude towards expansion is the key to the Sagittarian consciousness; he tries to expand on all levels, whether it be in

personality, learning, goals or relationships.

In Gemini and Cancer we learned of introverted/extroverted thinking and introverted/extroverted feeling respectively. In this and the following sign section I will discuss the Fiery and Earthy elements in terms of their subjective and objective components but it cannot be stressed too often that the psychological type does not necessarily equate with only the Sun in that particular element.

Sagittarius is often described as freedom-loving, honest, outgoing, clumsy, optimistic, jovial and sometimes a little less than tactful. There is, however, one major principle that lies behind all of the above outer characteristics: expansion. Like the other Fire signs, Sagittarians tend to be the lucky ones, a direct result of the intuitive function working at its best, coupled with the usual attitude of expectancy and vision. This attitude of expectancy derives from the psychological attunement to the intuitive function.

In the extroverted attitude it is characterized by one's orientation towards the activity of the outside world. Extroverted intuition often relies on hunches (from the unconscious) to which he directs his energies in the environment; he 'senses' something out there, acts on impulse and gingerly activates the situation while the impetus is still with him, acquiring a reputation for being impatient and over-hasty. He needs no logical, mechanical basis for his actions, he already 'knows' what he is going to do when he attempts something in the environment.

In its introverted function, the 'vision' is only part of his inner, subjective world, this produces the philosopher, creative artist and visionary who needs an outer object (often a canvas or writing book) on which to project his impressions.

Sagittarius is fun-loving and appears more than the other two Fire signs to be blessed by 'lady luck'. Many have attributed this to the Jupiter rulership and it does seem that help often arrives, if only at the eleventh hour. Their frequent good fortune is part and parcel of their psychologically expansive attitude. I have noticed that a great deal of Sagittarians are particularly tolerant of others around them, another aspect of 'putting back something into the object'. Having said that, they do shout their mouths off with alarming truthfulness and honesty, often completely unaware of their effect on others, that is until their victim is motionless with embarrassment. Scorpio, however, rather seems to enjoy this pursuit.

With Sagittarius on the cusp of a house, there is the same tolerant, expansive attitude towards the matters of that house, and it is here that one may receive the benefits of providence and good fortune.

Even taking these things for granted does not seem to cause much alarm.

Capricorn

With the second of the 'social' signs, we arrive at the tenth stage of the cycle. Man has now achieved union on an emotional level (Scorpio) and achieved the personal freedom that liberates him from the bonds of relationship (Sagittarius). A similar development is occurring as in the Aries–Taurus, Leo–Virgo progression when the selfness of the individual (Fire signs) is expressed more deliberately in realistic, practical terms (Earth signs).

In Capricorn the broad, philosophical view of the way in which other cultures and societies live their lives (Sagittarius) is brought down to earth and the individual now attempts to integrate himself within the social order. In this attempt he notices the various responsibilities he has whilst adapting himself to this society; certain rules must be observed, the requirements of the 'law-abiding citizen', and he learns that when laws are transgressed he must pay the penalty. Authority imposes certain regulations on his behaviour, certain acts are 'just not done' in public lest one invoke the moral condemnation of society.

Capricorn is particularly concerned about what others think of him when in the public eye. He must retain his dignity and propriety at all costs and often prefers to work 'behind the scenes' managing, directing and controlling.

In Taurus and Virgo we met the individual's development through physical needs, material security and the organization of one's practical affairs; in Capricorn man reaches the zenith of his personal ambitions, his own worldly concerns. This imbues Capricorn with an intense ambition, an instinctive perseverance and an ability to endure set-backs and frustration as if they were unconsciously testing themselves against the cruel winds of fate. Most of these set-backs occur early on in life and many a Capricorn has become more patient and stronger as a result, having learned that time is of the essence and all will surely come to those who wait.

This seriousness permeating the Capricorn consciousness is often given some light relief with their dry, tongue-in-cheek sense of humour. It is different from the sarcastic tongue of the Scorpio and the outspoken witticisms of Sagittarius; in Capricorn the humour is softer, more subtle and presented with a straight, serious face. Perhaps it is self-effacing humour, but if it is, it is a mask to cover their inner sense of nobility and grandeur. This aspect of Capricorn,

I believe stems from its association with the tenth house onto which is projected 'authority', 'prestige', 'social status' and 'honour'. The connection with Capricorn and the 'upper classes' or snobs of suburbia seems to have little to do with the essence of Saturn, which is the avoidance of human weakness in the unconscious, producing fear or the need to overcompensate.

In that case we have a mixture of social awareness and propriety (tenth house) and self-deprecation and uncertainty (Saturn) both rolled into one human being who can exude a desire to keep up with the Joneses, yet remain incredibly self-conscious and unsure of himself. Saturn does relate to the social order, but has nothing at all to do with prestige or social standing. In its fundamental application, Saturn 'rules' the structure of society as a whole, imposing laws and regulations on its members and requiring that they do the work necessary for it to function properly.

Capricorn fits the bill as a sensation type which appears to remain pure in the extroverted attitude. Sensation's function is to determine that something exists; extroversion is turning libido (psychic energy) towards objectivity. Therefore extroverted sensation is completely at home with material objects and the world of commerce and enterprise, since these things are fairly accessible and are able to bring the security he craves. He is probably good at manual work since he knows how to use his body and probably takes great pains to ensure a healthy diet, adequate exercise and decent attire. (In reference to the latter mention of clothing, the Earth signs do tend to dress conservatively.)

In its introverted attitude, the sensation arises from within and the outer object is not relied on for its supremacy. Sensations producing all manner of thoughts are drawn from the inner realm. For instance, two people may hear a piece of music but the sensations that they feel are entirely different. If this same couple are of introverted sensation, the inner perceptions and 'touches' cannot be relied on; one person simply won't hear something that the other person has heard and vice versa. The sensation function is to 'objectify' that 'something' yet we find this couple arguing over what it is they have heard. Neither of them are deaf; it is simply that they can only hear what they want to hear in their own subjective landscape.

With Capricorn on a house cusp you work hard in that area, think things through and shoulder responsibilities and it's hard luck if the breaks don't always come your way while you're young.

Aquarius

The eleventh phase in the zodiac is characterized by man's sense of collectivity, brotherhood and humanitarianism. Capricorn as the tenth sign is the pinnacle of worldly achievement and it is here that one's personal concerns come to an end. The following two signs have no such personal issues with which to contend. In Capricorn man has attained security and identity in the outside world and it truly appears that there is nowhere else left to go. In Aquarius, the personal attachments to the outer world are given over to the community for the good of the group, so we have the transition from personal ambition to collective ambition, from what is good for me and mine or my reputation to what is good for all of us, the world, the people as a whole.

It is from this group consciousness that Aquarius derives its outer nature, feeling at home in the company of friends, colleagues and associates, the more the better. It is also an Air sign and the third 'social' collective sign that began in Sagittarius and became adaptable to the demands of that society in Capricorn. The Aquarian, although fond of social pursuits and meeting people, sees no reason to adapt to current trends just because they are popular or prevailing.

This breaks down (or tries to break down) the structured unit to which Capricorn adhered. Aquarius is non-conformist and shares some of the love of freedom that is manifest in Sagittarius. The difference is that Sagittarius pursues freedom in order to experience as much of life as possible; thus it is freedom for its own sake. Aquarius' freedom is seemingly that with a means to an end. Aquarians believe in the rights of the individual, liberty for all, etc., but they insist on imposing their ideas on others because they believe they know the best possible way towards that liberation, hence the motivation towards politics and the restructuring of societies. Anything that imposes bounds, therefore, limits the freedom of the individual, and so we arrive at a paradox: 'We have ways of making you enjoy your freedom'. It is typical of the revolutionary to change the existing structure and reorganize it his way until it becomes a permanent fixture once again.

Aquarians are friendly creatures, though often erratic and unpredictable—sometimes even maniacal. This part of the Aquarian consciousness derives from the influence of Uranus, producing sudden, unexpected flashes of unpredictable behaviour. At a deeper level there is 'something in there' which strives for individuality and independence even though they feel alienated if cut off from the rest. They desire to be 'different' from the usual crowd, yet they need the crowd to relate to on an equal basis, another subtle paradox which is based on the Leo–Aquarius polarity.

They are often unconventional in their outward expression, indifferent to normally accepted standards, maintaining a cool, casual approach with an air of 'Couldn't care less'. But Aquarius cares deeply about humanity in general, and therefore often overlooks the individual. This is part of the reason why it is difficult for the Aquarian to become deeply involved with another on an emotional level. What will happen to his clear-headed rational mind? Aquarians then approach human situations in a spirit of friendly detachment; they need to have many friendships because for all their apparent indifference or eccentricity, they suffer from an inner lack of confidence in themselves as individuals.

On good days Aquarius can 'live and let live', allowing others the right to pursue their own lives, though they cannot resist offering some 'friendly advice'. With Aquarius on a house cusp, you desire freedom, independence and a certain detachment from the concerns in that area. Here you can be rationally minded, truthful, obstinate and perhaps just a little rebellious.

Pisces

Pisces completes the phase of the four social signs and ultimately the cycle of the zodiac itself. In the former role it brings people together, having dissolved all political issues of Aquarius. An archetypal Piscean type is the figure of Jesus, who taught us to love our neighbour as ourself. It is often a humble, self-sacrificing sign into which much of the Christ's values are woven. As the last stage in human unfolding, it represents an end of individual struggle and the ego often slips out of focus in the face of something or someone greater.

Pisceans can be extremely submissive, giving in to others when they really ought to have said 'no'. In true chameleon-like fashion, they are able to adapt to the needs and personality of their partner, camouflaged into the background, playing the willing servant. It is questionable whether or not this is an actual weakness. The Pisces gains his sensitive, impressionable nature from the Watery element in his psychological make-up and is able not only to understand, but actually feel what another feels in true empathetic style. Often the Piscean experiences such feelings as if they were coming from himself when in fact he has picked up on someone else's strong vibrations, and in time will come to resemble that person in style and mannerism if exposed to them for any lengthy period.

As a feeling type he is able to see the human qualities in the world around him. Understanding others as he does, it is difficult to shock him with something that you may have considered sensational or a scandal. What motivates the Piscean is the need to reach out to others and encompass life on a feeling level. Remember that in the cycle of the twelve signs, man's personal development towards individual gain ended after Capricorn, so that Pisces feels so strongly about contact with others that he often forgets himself and his own needs in favour of the partner.

I have met many Pisceans who are all too willing to share themselves and what they have with you in order to be appreciated or better still, loved. This is because Pisces has a poor sense of self and it is a great pity to see such people devaluing their own individuality in place of those close to them. It is at worst, a form of self-annihilation. At best it is the Piscean devotedness and kindness that is non-judgemental and takes consideration of the human values of the person concerned.

To understand something, noticing its emotional or perhaps sentimental value is to imbue it with a kind of 'little personality' as if it really lived (feeling). Contrariwise, to perceive something detachedly or clearly and place it in the 'scheme of things' i.e. its relationship to everything else of a similar nature (thinking) removes its personal value as existing with its own idiosyncrasies. Herein lies the difference between Pisces as a feeling type and Aquarius as a thinking type.

The easiest way for Piscean sensitivity to become twisted and clouded is the descent into self-pity, with enough complaints to make the individual's life sound like a soap-opera tragedy. They can be weak-willed and lazy enough to let someone else run their lives for them while they relax in a private paradise of fantasy and day-dreams; they might feel better off as a character in a romantic, housewife's bedtime novel.

This apparent nebulousness is part and parcel of the inner urge to reach out and dissolve boundaries, accentuated in its polar opposite of Virgo, where the boundaries of the real world are paramount; objects must be distinct, black and white and have a practical purpose to serve. Virgo acquires the necessary skills in order to deal with such everyday reality, subduing personality in favour of the object. Pisces has no such practical concerns and even though Pisceans (like the Virgoans) have a poor sense of individuality, the subject is the main criterion for them, homing in on the instinctual needs and moods of those around them, gaining their sense of identity by attachment to other people. The reclusive types who go to find God in a monastery or on a mountaintop in Tibet are still reaching out for something, that divine, energy-force that permeates the whole of nature—these are the Pisceans who have realized long ago that we can never be completely and utterly alone after all, and off they go to seek their guiding light.

The house with Pisces on its cusp is the one where you can get by with just a little help from your friends. You give plenty here and blend in effortlessly with the scenery.

4.
PLANETARY ARCHETYPES

The mere word 'archetype' may be unfamiliar and even harder to imagine as having a shape, size or form. When we speak of archetypes in depth psychology, we are discussing the original type of model through which human urges and motivations can be expressed. Such values permeating human nature can also be found in fables and proverbs, and in common parlance we speak of the proverbial 'stick in the mud' and as adults we are well aware of what is meant. We also hear talk of the archetypal 'jack of all trades' and once again, this sort of language finds it way into our understanding much quicker than trying to describe the inner urges associated with Taurus and Gemini.

Archetypes can thus be described in terms of planetary symbolism, although an archetype is not the same as a symbol. For instance, Saturn is the archetypal great teacher and Lord of Karma, distributing just desserts, teaching by experience. Therefore it points to something specific. In a sense there are as many archetypes as there are human situations, but the actual model is more or less a permanent fixture.

The archetypal hero, magician, trickster, sinner, saint, mother, father, etc., are all represented by human beings here and now in one form or another, painting a picture of the inner motivation they represent. They are subject to the usual human urges that are more or less common to us all. Therefore, one has an image of the teacher archetype and a pre-formed maze of associations immediately link us to what we understand as the archetypal teacher. One may use a particularly scholarly friend to embody the idea—and Saturn is probably strong in that person's chart. Thus it is presented in the form of an image, immediately expressing itself via a picture or an action with which we associate certain qualities. What is not so immediate is the symbol, for there is always something behind its obvious meaning and unlike the archetype it is inexhaustible in content.

Saturn is symbolized by a sickle and straight away, that sharp, inanimate object finds a response via a host of associations. To some it symbolizes the reaping of what one has sown during a lifetime, to others it may mean actual death and the cutting of the cord of fate. Not only the object iself and its obvious use is represented by the symbol; a sickle is a sharp, pointed object, so to some it may symbolize 'sharpness of behaviour', brittleness and one-pointedness, pointing one's energies to one aim in life, reminiscent of the behaviour of Saturn's Sun-sign, Capricorn. We could not talk of a 'sickle' archetype, because the actual object has no intention other than its own existence, but still on the subject of Saturn–Capricorn, we could propose an 'ambition archetype' or 'fear archetype' or put another way, the archetypal 'man at the top' or 'cowardly lion'.

The Sun, an Aspect of the Self

Looking at the Sun in a chart shows the regulating centre from which the person is operating and closely connects with the ordering pattern of 'fated' events through a person's life that Jung terms the 'Self'. If we ask ourselves, 'Where is this person going in life?' the answer will depend on all of the governing factors in that person's environment, not only his surrounding world, but his inner self.

The self, as Jung points out, cannot be reduced to final description, since, as he says, 'it does not predicate its own existence'. The self, then, relies on the innate predisposition of the individual, and what he does with those qualities he has been born with. It is like a book that has not yet been written. Once an individual looks back and reflects on his life's situations and experiences, he may see in retrospect what was written or a plan that he had unwittingly been following. The self is the unseen intelligence that somehow governs his life pattern of 'things that were meant to happen'. It's a kind of dim awareness that those events contained in life were not quite so random and meaningless after all.

The only way that the self could be appropriately described is the whole of the chart itself, that is, every last detail and the way in which the person has come to terms with the energies involved throughout a whole lifetime.

The Sun as a separate entity may point to the best course available. In simple terms, it shows one's talent, the creative side of us that if developed will shine like the Sun itself. The Sun in Taurus is creative with money, Sun in Gemini creative with words, Sun in Cancer, creative at home and so on.

The Sun as the Animus

Man is usually predisposed towards assertion, independence, action and will-power, or at least that's what the gossip press would have us believe. These qualities are part of the male principle, which is outgoing and directed towards objects. Represented in say, mythology, it is the driving force behind the Greek heroes, like Jason, Heracles and Perseus. It is achieving one's ends by action and initiative or if necessary, brute force. On every birth chart, then, there is a combination, often an imbalance of so-called positive, masculine energies and negative female energies. What then, of our quiet, polite, genteel young lady who, like everyone else, still has to contend with energies that are foreign to her natural make-up, which is one of relatedness. (Ever noticed how females often seem to make friends with another, almost instantly?)

Those masculine energies on her birth chart, primarily the Sun and Mars, may be awkward to express and alienated from her

Four Types of Animus

	Positive		*Negative*
FEELING (WATER)	Paternal	—	Limiting
	Protective	—	Emasculating
Poseidon/Neptune	Emotional	—	Unstable
	Compassionate	—	Cruel
THINKING (AIR)	Light	—	Superficial
	Co-operative	—	Manipulative
Hermes/Mercury	Clever	—	Unfeeling
	Dispassionate	—	Cold
SENSATION (EARTH)	Sensuous	—	Greedy
	Capable	—	Duty-bound
Cronus/Saturn	Earthy	—	Pedantic
	Appreciates	—	Enslaved to
	nature	—	senses
INTUITION (FIRE)	Creative	—	Unproductive
	Assertive	—	Domineering
Zeus/Jupiter	Energetic	—	Restless
	Heroic	—	Troublemaking

feminine psychology. They then combine to form an archetype, a second (or more likely a third) personality Jung calls the animus, the female fighting spirit. Woman's eternal image of what is masculine is dictated to her by the animus, but from where does it first spring?

The Sun's position by sign and house is where one usually finds that same male principle about which we are talking. The girl's anima is first born out of relationship to her father or brother and the image is ingrained for the rest of her life. Even if there is no actual father present during upbringing, the image is formed by an 'expectation', an assumption of how males are, not necessarily how they are in themselves, but one's own experience of them. The image is thus projected onto an actual male in one's lifetime. (See Chapter 1.)

When looking at a female chart, you can gain an insight into the kind of man she is attracted to by the sign and house position of the Sun and Mars, and the aspects they receive.

The Moon—the Mother Archetype

All that is feminine and unconscious, that is to say, unexpressed within the male becomes an object of projection, suitably clothing an actual female in the life of an individual. The Moon is one's emotional grounding place, a base for one's deep personal feelings, a vessel in fact, very much like the personal unconscious. The personal unconscious acts like a repository for one's emotional experiences during the course of one lifetime and it can be found lurking in the fourth and twelfth houses of the chart. There are no hard and fast rules in astrology; we are dealing with unique individuals. So how are we to find our way through the maze of the above associated meanings?

Let's begin with childhood, since this is the stage of life when an individual starts collecting habits, learning about the basic functions of his body and recognizes the need, albeit unconsciously, for shelter and protection from the environment. The stages of babyhood leave a deep impression on us and it is from those early conditioning factors, i.e. the mother's influence, that we inherit the need for emotional security. The individual at this stage is in the process of being moulded in a particular way, according to the demands of the mother and we eventually inherit from her more than we care to realize. We *become* part of her.

Find the Moon on your chart and you find the mother. You also find where you'll feel better if the area of the chart is given expression. It shows you what it feels safe and comfortable to do because that area of life suggests protection, comfort and security. Feeling insecure is often a product of being cut off from that source of protection; if you pay attention to the emotional needs of the Moon and satisfy them, you'll sleep soundly at night.

What about the mother archetype then? Isn't this simply our own mother? When someone mentions the word 'mother', what are the images that it invokes? The mythical, archetypal mother is nature herself, primitive, passive, changeable and full of the protective waters of life, all-sustaining, enduring. Water will erode the greatest rock down to a grain of sand, but it may save your life too. The intrinsic value of the feminine is its very passivity, which is regarded as being inferior in modern society.

Let's not beat about the bush and simply say that the typical idea of 'mother' is that of a protective being, a provider of emotional support when life gets tough and we want to retreat from this cruel world. It's all too easy to project one's expectactions of 'mother' onto the actual parent in the hope of eliciting these qualities. It can thus be seen that the mother archetype is something shared by us all— everyone fosters their own idea of 'mother'.

The Moon as Anima

Nature's own process, 'mother earth' is the life-giver that precedes even man himself and 'lady luck' is the deliverer of bounty and good fortune; both are aspects of the power of the matriarch. That which can enchant man is portrayed in the image of luxurious feminity in literature, fantasy image and in this century, on celluloid in order to illustrate the subtle power of the feminine. The woman carrying the man's projection seems to possess all of the fatally attractive qualities coming from outside of himself, when in fact, he is coming face to face with the unconscious. The Moon and Venus on a male chart ably demonstrate the potential for growth through the anima, the qualities composed from these two planets by their chart positions make up the female element in man. The kind of woman he finds himself attracted to then, are those who resemble his Moon and Venus signs—as subtle directions from the anima lead him into relationship.

The anima archetype is man's inner face, the one that looks to the inner feminine world of receptivity and it is often the outwardly strong and domineering male who is weak and submissive just underneath the surface. The psyche, as we have seen, strives for balance and union, and any imbalance will be paid for with the correct due, namely an intrusion into one's conscious world. Since feminine qualities cannot be easily admitted into male consciousness, they are left unguarded, down there in the unconscious. But they try, as is their wont, to express themselves, taking the line of least resistance. Since they are being 'resisted' by the male conscious mind, they surface in projection, as a new energy to their rightful abode—but is it?

All males have certain expectations of the female role during relationships; here is the expressive function of the anima archetype—he 'knows' how women are, but he knows in fact, only of his own experiences of the female and the legacy left by the psychological impressions of the mother.

Anima Types

	Positive	*Negative*
FEELING (WATER)	Maternal	— Devouring
	Warm	— Cold
Artemis/Diana	Mysterious	— Nebulous
	Sensitive	— Neurotic
THINKING (AIR)	Communicative	— Superficial
	Youthful	— Vain
Aphrodite/Venus	Butterfly-like	— Vacuous
	Adaptable	— Fickle
SENSATION (EARTH)	Sensual	— Abandonment to physicality
	Practical	— Hard-headed
Gaia/Mother Earth	Aesthetic	— Emphasis on possessions
	Productive, fertile	— Lacks vision
INTUITION (FIRE)	Changeable	— Lacks stability
	Optimistic	— Flighty
Athena/Minerva	Independent	— Brash
	Self-centred	— Egotistical

Mercury and the Conscious Mind

The gifts of intelligence have been elevated to such a position that anyone possessing nine 'A' levels and a doctorate may be considered a genius. He may also be an emotional clod. That is to say that when the emphasis is on intellectual abilities, the gifts of the heart go unrecognized.

Mercury is an asexual figure in the Greek pantheon; that is, he is neither exclusively masculine nor feminine. He is completely cold in his evaluations and relies on weighing one set of facts against another, the great filtering processor of the zodiac. He seeks out information and applies meaning to it for the purpose of recognition. The data is fed into the computer and out come the results. It all sounds like an equation with no purpose, other than to know—or create—sense out of a random number of chaotic events.

Mercury's urge is to communicate something which we wish to express and therefore it sets in motion a process of synthesis and integration. Often it is the process that provides a channel for whatever information is stored. The channel may be one's voice, putting pen to paper or picking up the phone, and here is the fundamental process of the Mercury archetype—the two-way process of distribution and accumulation of information. That is one of the keys to its androgynity. It receives and it gives out; the simple act of merely looking around one's own living room, using only one's eyes, is a Mercury function, one of the conscious brain's, but that is not to say that Mercury fits hand in glove with the experiences contained in consciousness.

Seeing is a Mercury function, and so are the functions incorporated into it. The object of one's vision is communicated back to the individual and is recognized as such. For instance, if one observes a book on the table opposite, one recognizes the object as 'book', because we have given it a name and reality, because it is experienced as being distinct in shape and size from everything else in the room, except of course, other books. It also has a certain hue, which we define as colour and we go so far as to give that colour a name and say brown, because to our eyes it is different from black.

Can you recognize all of the mechanisms that have evolved through this Mercury function? On the surface, I can say that I know I have a mind because I am conscious of myself and can recognize things, but below that are the functions of the sense organs.

Back in our living room we note that a brown book, about eight inches in length is lying on the table in front of the red velvet drapes beside the new video-recorder that was delivered last Tuesday. Immediately these things occur to us, it takes little effort on our part to realize them. We don't have to strain ourselves to think of these things anymore, it's as if something was operating on a twenty-four-hour shift all our lives. This is the conscious mind, the pilot-light function that guides us through the simplest of efforts that we never stop to think about because they are so trivial.

The conscious mind is that function that is like a pilot-light that can be turned up to a fuller flame at will. When we try to think and make an effort to use our minds, it is like the semi-conscious process becoming fully conscious, either of object or subject. Therefore, the invisible functioning of one's mind, albeit conscious mind, is Mercury.

In my experience I have found that Mercury is very neutral and is only prominent when in strong aspect or on an angle. It would be misleading to say that Mercury represents 'the way your mind works' because the way one's mind works is governed by all of the chart. It would be better to assign it to the conscious mind and the filtering of information and facts for knowledge and distribution to others. The objects of one's environment are communicated back to us, via sight, sense, sound, etc., and immediately the mind gives us the relevant information, which we may or may not classify and store for further use. It is the device we employ to sift through the files of memory, but not the memory itself.

Venus—What Attracts You?

Apart from its association with the Anima as a female element of the male psyche, the Venus archetype represents man's driving towards relationship with another. There is an enigma about attraction because there is no accounting for taste. Venus on the birth chart demonstrates those influences in one's physical and emotional life that have a certain 'pulling power' about them; what is it exactly that turns you on?

Venus is the feminine strength that draws things to it without having to exert much force or will. What is this mysterious, powerful image that can leave us spellbound, perceived in the object of our affections? God, so they say, made man in his own image and likewise, an individual creates for himself images of other people corresponding to his own psychological make-up. We are all attracted to various types of human being and when we feel this 'pull' we are acknowledging the archetype. Whatever expression it takes depends on the Venus sign in the horoscope. As I have pointed out, the Moon and Venus symbolize the receptive nature in man (anima), and the Sun and Mars, the power of assertion and opinions in the female (animus). On her own, Venus means what one is generally attracted towards, the motivation in the arena of physical love and courtship, friendship, co-operation and perhaps the type of person you would consider marrying. Being turned on by physical attractiveness is Venusian—the vain one strikes again!

Mars—Who Needs a Hero?

Women fall in love with the embodiment of all that is masculine, and most removed from their usual consciousness. The animus is possessed of opinions; that is, prior assumptions and directness that is normally associated with masculine consciousness. When a woman becomes stubborn and immovable, when she plucks up the courage to fight and decides that she will 'get her own way' she has been visited by the animus. Remember Scarlett O'Hara's determination in *Gone with the Wind*? There are of course, ways of portraying this figure in literature; the hero of Emily Brontë's *Wuthering Heights*, Heathcliffe, is an excellent example of the ghostly power of the animus and there is such a variety of heroic figures through countless novels by such authors as Edgar Rice Burroughs, the Brontës and even Ian Fleming, that one could not possibly fail to miss the point.

Ladies, what kind of men do you admire? Look to your birth chart and note the Sun and Mars positions. Which houses are they in and what are the aspects? When you've finished reading this book you will have an idea of why you are only attracted to a certain type of man. Mars in Scorpio in the first? A secretive, mysterious battler who behaves the way you do. Mars in Libra in the tenth? A refined, polite talker engaged in his career and ambitions.

Mars on the birth chart needs some attention, if you are generally passive about things, that is, content to let things be. You may have a problem with anger and may be projecting Mars energy, unwittingly clothing others with the projection and letting them get aggressive for you. Remember, anything unconscious is projected and it may take more than a little self-realization and eye-opening to observe the beast that you've created. Why do you think it happens that a woman becomes involved in a relationship with an alcoholic or mentally disturbed male only to find that subsequent relationships turn out along similar lines? The well-publicized case of the woman who had a huge win on the football pools and said she was going to spend, spend, spend is an example of recurring projection.

The qualities one elicits through others repeatedly, do not fully belong to the other (object) and are a result of oneself (subject) disowning qualities that are felt undesirable. For a lot of people, anger is felt to be undesirable and this is the trouble encountered with the archetype of Mars, a fundamental energy of effort and 'having a go'. When there is an excess of this sort of energy, Mars is exaggerated and rides roughshod over everyone and everything. There is nothing intrinsically malefic about Mars; if the energy trying to find expression is suppressed we may encounter it through others and think that there's something out to get us. We really need to express all of the energies on the birth chart and allow room for them; there is no hope of 'overlooking them'. Trying to 'overcome' energies on the birth chart misses the point altogether. One cannot squash or restrain something that is living and moving like a continuous stream, for very long. Eventually, the dam bursts forth.

Jupiter—Faith Will Move Mountains—or so they Say

Next in line from the archetype of 'effort and trying' or male assertion is another masculine planet that together with Mars, has much to say about the processes underlying Jung's intuitive type. Intuition here, means an unconscious perception that is not too readily explained or given to reason but it is there nonetheless, often in a flash, like lightning which Jupiter ruled. The true essence of Jupiter is a simple faith which stands behind the archetypal image. It is fundamentally the same as intuition in its Jungian sense where the Fire signs are concerned. The faith archetype is expressed through the Fire signs and probably exemplified best through Sagittarius, always positive and freely optimistic concerning the outcome of things. There again, a keyword to this faith archetype—freedom. Being free means not being bound by circumstances and psychological freedom means the freedom to choose one's own thoughts, being aware of the reality of the now and liberated from the past.

Let's put this into a definite context: we said that Jupiter is a faith archetype. Faith used here does not mean the same thing as belief, belief in something is the result of some sort of conditioning and inevitably one is bound in some way to belief. Belief clings, it excludes any other possibility that does not fit in its framework. If I firmly believe in the doctrines of a Jehovah's Witness, I cannot believe in Krishna. If I believe that man descended from apes, I cannot believe that he was fashioned out of dust. Faith on the other hand is a genuine love of nature itself, a faith in the changefulness of the universe and when life becomes dull or depressive, a simple faith that the present period is only transitory.

What we are talking about then, is blind faith, a faith which requires no reasoning, no conditions and not even any attempt at thinking. It is therefore a general, faithful expectancy of life, like the intuitive concerned with the possibilities inherent in a situation. Occultists will tell you that to expect something is to precipitate its happening. Why do you think that the Fire signs are luckier than the rest of us? They haven't considered the possibility of failure—

and that is the secret of their success.

We take more things for granted than we realize. We take it for granted that the food we eat will be digested, we expect that when we stand on two feet and move one in front of the other we will be able to walk, but we have little faith in the more intangible things of life. Jupiter helps us to have that faith.

The area where Jupiter is found on your chart makes sure that you're protected and allowed plenty of breathing space. You will be lucky there in some way and the psychological processes that have just been explained bring you that luck. In psychological parlance, one would say that the individual attracts these fortunate experiences into his life by way of an unconscious process that is activated through expecting its very happening.

What one thinks, one will create, and I'm sure that you will have noticed at least one of the countless paperbacks, mostly by American authors, that extol the virtues of the 'power of the subconscious mind' and explain how to get rich through the aid of mental suggestion. With Jupiter, it is the 'taking for granted' (which is the same as 'having blind faith in something') that 'causes' us to be lucky. Astrology tells us that its principle is that of expansion and growth and that it is the greater benefic; depth psychology will tell us that it is the archetype for blind faith, and the Great Father.

Jupiter as the 'God' Archetype

The Sun is the principal regulating centre of the chart and a vessel for the archetype that Jung calls 'the self' which must precede all other symbols. The self is the 'X' factor on the chart because it cannot be reduced to a single element in astrology; the self is the lifetime of the whole chart, the manifestation of the planetary energies as they appear through meaningful events in one life. It is then, a nucleus, a germ of something not already born whose meaning is seen before, during and after the event. It is all at once its potential, manifest energy and by-product because they are all part of the same thing just as the Sun is related to the rest of the chart.

The self is the creative unfolding of a chart that is tied to fate; therefore it is significant in the life of an individual, it is the path that he has 'chosen' and at the same time 'had chosen for him'. Whatever one's idea of God, one cannot escape natural events; one is just as much a part of nature as the landscape, subject to the cycle of change that ends with death. The Jupiter myth in some ways has a theme similar to that of the Judaeo-Christian God and its battle with the forces of evil, in the form of Lucifer.

The opposite figure to Zeus/Jupiter in this context would be Cronus/Saturn. In traditional astrology, one brings good luck, providence and joy, while the other can only manage bad luck, limitation and sorrow. There is a strong link with Satan, as the Shadow, the bringer of evil through sensual, earthly pleasure, and Saturn. There is a similar one with God, as the great, protective father, gleaming with the light of wisdom, concerned with spiritual, heavenly enlightenment, and Jupiter.

These images are the ones fostered by Christian doctrine and serve to illustrate the polarity of Jupiter and Saturn in astrological reference. The 'God' archetype must be that of the masculine perpetrator of all things considered 'good'. That certainly applies when discussing the effect of Jupiter on the chart. There is also a strong religious element to Jupiter; philosophy being the religion of modern man. The Jupiter archetype is man's striving for wisdom, via a genuine, even childlike faith. As a masculine 'God' archetype it is protective of others, generous and genuinely creative, tireless in its positive efforts and optimism; whereas on the seventh day, the other God rested.

Saturn—What Are You Really Afraid Of?

I'd like to repeat that question, 'What are you really afraid of?' in order to draw attention to the beast of traditional astrology, the planet that has recieved so much bad press throughout the ages. Of course, we know a little better now, because we can say, 'You will experience certain limitations and frustrations from which you will learn a great deal, thus handling your life better the next time around. During the next month you may undergo serious changes in your circumstances, or encounter break-ups in your personal life.' But it doesn't make the situation any less painful and it is typical of today's astrologer to express a basic psychological process clothed in such vague, colourless terms as 'serious changes' in order not to elicit the usual reactions that the mere word Saturn brings.

Jupiter is the archetype of faith; here is where you 'let go' and trust in life, and therefore where you are lucky. Saturn equals fear, equals 'hanging on', equals bad luck. It's really as simple as that. It is the game of trying to structure reality according to your own illusion of it. For life to be natural, it must flow, like a river; Saturn is the area on the chart where you are likely to be hung up on control, you don't seem to be able to let go and allow this natural flow to happen. No wonder there is a negative outcome. Life is change, the universe is in a state of permanent flux; that must also include human beings, not only their physical bodies but their experiences too. Life is built around relating, to others and back to oneself, therefore relationships are subject to this same process of transformation; a relationship only ends, therefore dies, when there is no life left in it. Human beings are perpetually trying to structure areas of their life without recognizing the fact of change. They say that they want security; have you ever found any security in your relationships? The Saturn archetype is that within us that tries to contain and mould our experiences into a crystallized unit. In many ways it is trying to build and accumulate.

This trying to 'structure nature' is futile, for as I have pointed out, there are no guarantees on what will happen tomorrow; everything changes. Saturn represents, in some part, this striving for security—yet this very striving is likely to have an undermining effect, the opposite of what is intended.

To strive for something permanent then—say, a relationship, a career, a marriage—is to try to negate insecurity. We hope that once we have secured our relationship, our career, our marriage, all our fears will suddenly disappear. It is only the intention of actually making these things permanent structures that invites a feeling of anxiety and fear, and therefore pain. Pain is inherent in the accumulative process, in the fear of loss, the fear of losing what one has patiently built up over the years.

With Saturn we depend on succeeding at something so much, it is little wonder that we become cautious and serious during the process. Dependency on something or someone has fear at its root. How are we to cope without them? Whenever there is an emotional investment in something, one is dependent on succeeding, the more one holds on to the reins, the more unsympathetic one becomes to one's human flaws and shortcomings, and the more one has a horror of failing. This is Saturn at its worst, but the root of this unfortunate behaviour is still there where you find Saturn on the chart. In your Saturn areas you demand to be in control. The seriousness arises as we have said from a strong emotional investment in succeeding, thereby ignoring human weaknesses and often hating ourselves for them. This self-effacing attitude is a by-product of ignorance; we are not prepared to allow for silly little fears or to admit our inadequacies, so we chastise ourselves for being too weak, and this is why Saturn is called the great taskmaster.

All this self-control blocks the flow of life and we become afraid to be afraid. It is not the fear itself that causes the problem; it is the reluctance to admit that we're afraid at all. After all, what are you really afraid of?

Saturn as the Shadow

It is natural for human beings to compensate in some way for their sore spots. The usual reaction is to ignore the awkward area altogether and pretend it doesn't exist. But that does not make it go away, indeed, shutting it away in a dark cupboard only enrages it even more. The personification of man's instinctual, animal nature, encompassing all manner of primitive urges and so-called 'evil' tendencies, Jung termed the Shadow. Man's 'Mr Hyde' nature seeks expression, with the same urge to fulfilment on the horoscope. Look to Saturn on the birth chart and you will have a pretty good idea of how the Shadow archetype is likely to manifest. The Shadow is the natural enemy of the ego as the unconscious material compensates in direct proportion to those qualities that have been attached to the ego. The theme of polarity and balance is repeated here.

The more one strains to be 'good' and 'pleasant', the more the thing that would negate those qualities accumulates in the unconscious. As one strives to express the best in oneself; generosity, good humour, co-operativeness, etc., the psyche, needing to maintain equilibrium imbues the Shadow with the dark, other half of those qualities which have been grafted onto the ego. These disowned contents become projected on to others who in some way appear to qualify for the shadowy overcoat with which we are going to fit them. They are the embodiment of everything we despise and consider alien to our own nature.

Look at the Saturn area on your chart to see the qualities you may be projecting and heaping out on to an unfortunate neighbour. Having imbued the ego with the pleasant qualities of generosity, co-operation and humour, the opposites that the Shadow contains— selfishness, non-cooperation and seriousness, fall onto any object capable of carrying the projection. But however successful the projection, the Shadow follows you wherever you go.

What if we were to permit ourselves a little understanding of our Saturn Shadow natures and think of all the qualities that we dislike in others? This would involve revising our interpretation of the root causes of these dislikes. Most of these roots are in fear. Suppose we discover that we have an intense dislike of individuals who are selfish, jealous, hypocritical, peevish and bombastic (who doesn't?). We then find one word at the root of all these descriptions of character: fear.

The selfish person is afraid to be generous to others; often he cannot even be generous to himself, and he has little trust in human nature. The jealous person is afraid of losing something very precious to him, afraid of someone else taking this precious satisfaction away from him. The hypocritical person does not trust his own judgement, he is afraid to admit the truth to himself and others. The peevish type is like the jealous one, afraid of losing his possessions, afraid of ending up with nothing. The bombastic person is afraid of himself, he needs to make a bigger noise than the rest simply to impress himself. He is afraid of being powerless, so he bullies others weaker than himself in order to perpetuate his stance.

Here is a table of Shadow qualities, grouped in elements that may provide some understanding of the projection.

Shadow Types

Saturn in	Root	Projection
AIR	Weak intellectual ability	Hates 'smart Alecs'
	Slow mental reactions, slow learner	Hates being beaten to the punch
	Thorough in reflection	Hates scatterbrains
	Lacks spontaneity	Avoids intellectual conversation and debate
WATER	Emotionally stunted	Dislikes 'gushy' types
	Strict domestic life	Envious of those who 'had it too easy'
	Blocked feelings	Hates people showing emotion
	Lacks human values	Dislikes 'soft touches'
EARTH	Bound to duties	Envious of ambitious successful business types
	Possessive, cautious	Dislikes spendthrifts
	A means to an end	Jealous of those with money to burn
	Shy concerning physical body	Envious of good looking people
FIRE	Suppresses individuality	Hates 'bigheads' and 'show-offs'
	Lacks self-confidence	Avoids 'arty' types
	Self-expression blocked	Avoids overbearing types
	Lacks vitality	who 'burn people out'

Uranus, Neptune, Pluto and the Collective Unconscious

The three outermost planets, Uranus, Neptune and Pluto represent energies that are removed from consensus reality—that is, factors in one's make-up that are somehow above and beyond so-called everyday reality. The first five planets symbolize man's inner-self, emotional needs, means of communication, urge to relate and capacity for action and are respectively the Sun, Moon, Mercury, Venus and Mars. The next two Jupiter and Saturn, are collective forces whereby the individual may grow beyond himself and observe life as a structured unit.

These seven planets gain access into consciousness simply because they are 'all too human'. Even animals possess the functions from the Sun through to Mars. Most people have difficulty handling Saturn energies, let alone transpersonal figures such as the big three. It is often said that these planets act on a collective level, affecting a whole generation who share the same sign position of the particular body. We hear talk of the Pluto in Leo generation, and how it gave rise to drastic changes in values about one's children. The Pluto in Cancer generation has suffered the pains of family separation through the atrocities of a world at war. How do these unconscious, transforming energies affect the individual?

During Jung's research into the psyche, he 'uncovered' a bottom layer beneath the personal unconscious where the psychic history of man had been written, as though carved with a knife into a tree. In the same way that we inherit the genes of our forefathers, so have we inherited the ways and means by which they existed. What we are talking about here is primitive man, the man that was left behind as civilization gained speed and burst forth into the twentieth century. The man who was limited in knowledge but not in his own simple wisdom. The simple wisdom that modern man has somehow lost in this crazed, technological rat-race we call living. The remnants of this precious age are still with us, lying deep in the unconscious. The foundations of man's psyche, since we presumably came from the same source, have their roots in what Jung termed the Collective Unconscious. It is as if we have part of us that connects to the Infinite or God, or whatever you prefer to call it. The planets Uranus, Neptune and Pluto connect us to energies that are beyond everyday experiences, a sort of divine reservoir. This reservoir is right there in the unconscious mind though, and its effects are most strongly felt at crisis periods when the energies of the three outer planets are triggered off.

It is commonplace for modern man to cling to his little securities, his job, his car, his family, and generally create a safe, sound existence for himself. Succumbing to the utilitarian notion that 'this is the way life is lived', he has carved out a life in such a way that he cannot think of himself existing in any other fashion. Put simply, man tends to resist change.

If the above leanings towards security remind you very much of Saturn, that is because they are. They are the Saturn principle exemplified in terms of material security and dependence on objects. When the structure becomes too tight, Uranus appears with a sledgehammer and shatters it to fragments. Ruling Aquarius as it does, Uranus makes its children feel as if they were living on a different planet, somehow cut off from mundane life and the area where Uranus is found on the chart represents this sphere of behaviour. It shows where you need to be different in terms of uniqueness of individuality. The archetype that all at once seems removed from everyday reality, lying and waiting in the collective unconscious, often provides a welcome break from the routines and ordinariness of daily living. That is Uranus' greatest gift; it blesses an individual with honesty, uniqueness and unconventionality, granting an opportunity to express his independence according to his wont.

Wherever Uranus is found on the chart there is a wilfulness and desire for independence to some degree, often reacting vehemently against anyone who tries to stand in the way or impose authority. Uranus rebels when the situation has become suffocated with orders and demands from the outside and its revolt in the psychological sense is the unconscious suddenly demanding freedom for itself. The conscious mind has 'held on' for too long and suddenly there bursts forth the unconscious need for freshness and vitality.

When Uranus energies manifest, they do so suddenly. There is something within us that needs to be free and express independence, namely the Uranus area on your chart and the house that has Aquarius on its cusp. There have been revolutions in one form or another throughout the course of history, human beings trying to overthrow those who would flaunt their power; this uniqueness of character has been with man always. He is and always has been—an original model.

It is said that when God made man, he threw away the mould and started again. If Uranus doesn't give a damn about what others think of him, then Neptune cares very much indeed, and suggests that, unlike Uranus, we all spring from the same mould. Deep down in the collective unconscious, there is a dim awareness of the divine, mystical and spiritual. It can be perceived in such reactions as fascination, awe and even ecstasy as one looks into the scarlet sunset over the ocean or at a beautiful summer night's sky filled with stars.

The collective unconscious may be likened to that of the deepest part of the sea, where some of its contents eventually find their way to the shore, washed up onto the beach (conscious mind) after many years. People change as they mature and find themselves doing and saying things they would never have conceived of ten years earlier. Neptune's link to the collective unconscious is that half-hearted longing for the ideal and the notion that there is 'something more than this', 'something out there'. It is the spiritual perception of the universe, as opposed to Saturn's material conception of ordered reality. Put simply, Neptune rules another order of reality, the things one experiences on planes other than the material. For instance, where do your dreams take place? Obviously, you had experienced a particular 'stage setting' and remembered certain locations, some even familiar, but what was it that produced the dream? If we give it a name and call it the unconscious, we will probably assume that the unconscious has a life of its own, independent of the conscious mind as well as compensating for the discarded contents of the ego.

Neptune rules those so-called psychic states, of which the dream is one. It does not happen in the 'here and now' so to speak, so it must happen somewhere else. My own conception of 'reality' is that whatever it is you have ever experienced must be real, if only to you. If it happened to you, it must have been real. This does not mean that it actually existed in tangible form, but since it became part of your conscious awareness, it existed for you.

This is the ground we are intruding on when we discuss Neptune, in many ways the antithesis of Saturn. Wherever Neptune is on the chart, there is often an idealism about that area not found anywhere else, depending on how unconscious of Neptune you are. One sticks the imagery into that Neptune area with a vague intention to achieve something, forever indecisive. You can run the gauntlet of martyrdom, succumbing to the whims of others, being treated in much the same way as a doormat. Or your compassion for others can relieve suffering, dissolving the walls that people build around themselves, calling for gentleness, kindness and some good old-fashioned sympathy.

One of Neptune's positive faces is that it will give of itself. It tends to soak up the prevailing influences around when there are strong energies from others, drawing the atmosphere of the environment into itself, so it represents that within us that connects us to the infinite, the unconscious depths from where we sprang. In the unconscious there are no boundaries, everything is in a state of potential, the ideal state in its shifting fluidity. Neptune tries to attain that ideal state here on earth, but the finite can never perceive the infinite fully enough. Hence the reputation for vagueness, dreaminess, self-deception, sneakiness and the rulership over drugs and alcohol. Escapism is one way at least to achieve that ideal state; sensation through stimulating drugs and alcoholic drink is an appropriate, even inexpensive vehicle. Neptune in the collective unconscious represents the way in which man has longed for a god since time immemorial, the divine longing for an all-powerful father, the promise of shelter, embraced in his loving and forgiving arms, that is archetypal. One only needs to read the Christian Bible to see the idea at work. Therefore it is that within us that captures a dim awareness of the 'one-ness with the universe', unity and the feeling that God is in fact alive, well, and living in the twentieth century.

The cycle of nature is an unending pattern of changes—spring arrives with the Vernal Equinox, plants are ready to push forth through the soil, trees are contemplating having leaves once more. The Summer Solstice arrives whilst the Sun enters Cancer, the flowers have bloomed, the trees are doing very nicely and people book foreign holidays to take advantage of the warm weather. All very pleasant. What is not so pleasant for individuals is the thought of it all too soon drawing to a completion, an end, having outgrown its usefulness. The brilliant sheen of life's pleasures tarnishes under its own desire to perpetuate eternal this or that, trying to hold on to the experience and make it last.

Pluto demands that when anything has outlived its potential it must be laid on the altar of sacrifice to be ceremoniously annihilated. Even some of us who do not perform such rites on a daily basis, acknowledge the need for growth and the 'killing off' of a particular situation that has become dull and stale with the passing of time. The situation that is not eliminated only festers and creates a terrible smell for the individual concerned, like blocked drains. A plumber can unblock a drain with relative ease, but it becomes a little more strenuous for humans to let go of outworn, disintegrating parts of their own lives. People often try to hang on to stale marriages or relationships; 'better the devil you know than the devil you don't'. It is not only limited to this sphere; one's career or home life may become excruciatingly monotonous and boring until the point is reached when something drastic has to be done.

The Pluto archetype then, is one of the power of transformation, the birth–life–death sequence permeating the soul of mother nature herself from which there is no escape. It is better to let certain things die, creating a space for new life to be built in its place. This is the essence of Pluto, lord of the hidden, unseen, land of the dead. It is a subtle but infinitely powerful energy, rising from the unconscious that creates such irrevocable change and one that the preserves of modern reality are out of touch with. Yet, that unbelievable power is within us, somewhere, part of man's collective psychological origins.

It all depends on what you do with that power. Tapping into such a force and using it to manipulate one's own ends or worse, manipulate others, is a questionable pursuit indeed and borders on the realms of black magic. The position of Pluto, like Uranus and Neptune, is one that links us with the transpersonal world of the collective unconscious. It is the area on the chart that is subject to the 'dying-off and being reborn' process, often re-shuffling our values about that part of lives and providing a vehicle for Plutonian power. We may 'kill something off' psychologically, annihilating old, negative thought processes, freeing the way for more faith and trust in nature. We may eliminate old habit patterns, thus cleaning up our act and dying to the past. Therefore it is a process of purification. Look to Pluto on your chart and you may well find these transformations have been going on 'behind your back'. That is because of its hidden, often subversive nature and true to its astrological behaviour, the actual planet Pluto hides from the prying eyes of even the most technologically advanced telescopes.

Man's unconscious motivation towards the need for renewal, therefore the death of part of himself, is echoed in the activities of Pluto on the natal chart. We are really speaking of a metaphorical death, such as the ending of a relationship, even the dissolution of a corporation. These 'little deaths' can be seen every day, if you take the trouble to look for them, for remember that Pluto loves to hide.

5.

THE DIVISIONS OF THE HOROSCOPE

Your Rising Sign/Persona and the Horoscope Angles

The saying goes that all the world's a stage, and this may have special psychological significance when you consider the projection of your own moods onto an external situation. In moments of anxiety, under the influence of tension and stress, the whole world it seems, fills us with misgivings that only appear to back up our belief that everything is against us. Similarly when we feel good, the world seems to be on our side and everything goes well for us. There are some days when it seems 'nothing will go right' and on the other hand when 'nothing will go wrong'. Why do you suppose this is so? Are we really so much separated from the external situation?

The rising sign is that one ascending on the eastern horizon at the moment of birth and marks the point where the earth meets the heavens, or where the inner reflects the outer, or expressed in more literal terms, where our view of the outside world is coloured by our own personal, inner world. It is a lens which we use to focus our impressions upon so-called external reality; everything we see is coloured by the energies of the rising sign and likewise this information is transmitted back to us so that it represents the face or mask which we present to the world in order to adapt to outer conditions, performing the same function as the persona. The sign on the ascendant is often much more obvious on first encountering anyone than is the Sun-sign, since it often alters considerably one's physical and facial characteristics and personal mannerisms which one wishes to display. Although it is not really a matter of 'wishing', the contents of the rising sign are quite natural and spontaneous.

In technical terms, the rising sign is the sign on the cusp of the first house; the sign opposite then becomes the cusp of the seventh house. In the calculation, the chart is then subdivided into quadrants by another axis, forming eastern and western hemispheres in addition to north and south, formed by the ascendant–descendant axis. The first–seventh house axis pertains to one's relationships in general; the fourth–tenth axis marks the wholly individual, personal life of the individual, the roots from which he sprang and the worldly achievements to which he will direct his energies. As in the ascendant--descendant relationship, these are two ends of the same scale and it is up to the individual to try to bridge the gap if he is to achieve a working harmony throughout life. The angle that begins the fourth house is the *Imum Coeli* or IC; its opposite point, the *Medium Coeli* or MC is the true cusp of the tenth house and this has come to be known as the 'parents axis', providing information about one's roots, domestic life and attitude towards authority figures.

In juxtaposition to one's relationship to the environment (ascendant/descendant) there is one's own, inner personal life, the emotional base from which one operates. One cannot perform satisfactorily in one's job if there are insecurities and anxieties lurking beneath the surface and it is only when the matters of the fourth house are in good working order that one is able to operate happily and freely in the environment. Thus it is a concern for emotional security, building a feeling base within oneself that is at the foundations of the fourth house. If it is on rocky ground, the support system is in danger of collapsing and the emotional life becomes unsteady and nervous. The need for a base is translated into material terms; when one acquires a home, a stretch of land, 'something to call my own' so that it becomes symbolic of one's need for an inner base, the inner is merely projected onto the outer.

Once again we are projecting an inner psychic state onto an object that reflects our personal, unconscious images, because all of the contents which we either find fascinating or repellent in the outside world are reflections from the world within us. Our feelings about something in the world around us have their counterpart in the mind. There is little difference between the world and one's experience of it, since this experience is all that can truly be said to exist.

The world is only there as it appears to you; to look out upon a sunny sky and experience a joyous feeling is to 'be' that feeling, for there is no separating you from what you feel. Perhaps this sounds a little obscure, but in moments of joy and ecstasy, you 'are' that joy and there is no attempt to be separate from it; in fact it is not even possible to expel certain feelings as if they can somehow be shown the door or refused admittance. Look at what happens when we try: the feeling does not go away simply because we deny its presence. In addition we are inviting friction and tension when we attempt to resist our inner thoughts and feeling sensations.

These inner dramas are played out in the fourth house, far removed from its polar opposite, the tenth. At the cusp of the tenth house is the MC, which says something about 'where you are going in life', your worldly aim or objective, and this axis is intensely personal in contrast to the ascendant–descendant axis. It denotes a path of individual striving, from early on in life to the moment one retires, and is the world that one attends to for oneself, from your personal feelings base of operations to the activities you identify yourself with on the long road to personal fulfilment.

Ascendant-Descendant Axis
Relating to the world in general, as opposed to one-to-one relationships. Aspects of oneself that are spontaneously produced (one's natural expression), as opposed to aspects of oneself that are spontaneously produced by projecting them onto others (one's natural expectations of others). One's relationship to oneself and relationships with others. Qualities we are usually conscious of and qualities we are often unconscious of.

Fourth House (IC) v Tenth House (MC) Axis
One's identification with something in the inner world; and in the outer world. Experiences we have brought with us (childhood); and those we are striving for (adulthood). Qualities we wish to hide (feelings, emotions); and those we wish to display and be known for. Maintaining one's inner, personal life; and one's outer, professional life.

The Astrological Theatre of the Houses
Take your seats ladies and gentlemen, around the circular stage. It's your show after all, the scenario in which you are all at once the director, producer, actor and audience. Each of the twelve stages are lit up to different degrees, some have been painted much brighter than others, some have a floating tapestry of different colours whilst others are in stark black and white. These are, my friends, the twelve astrological houses, representing various phases in life, repeating the same essential cycle produced through the signs.

If signs are styles or modes of experience, then the houses are an outer object on to which we project the planetary energies, providing a channel with the sign and a background scene with the house. In this theatre you will notice that the actors have a main performance to enact (planet) and the script tends to become slightly altered, according to whoever is reciting the words (sign). The play and the action take on a very different mood when the scenery has been changed (even though it is the same performer) and on finding himself on another stage in a different part of the theatre he will have taken on an entirely different role (house). Because the houses are another birth–death phase, when we are looking at the chart, we are looking at a cycle within a cycle, plotting the evolution of the actual signs and the stages of life that man finds himself in at the given moment.

The stages have thus been set. Some of them are tenanted by more actors and actresses than others and inevitably your gaze falls upon them more often than the odd, dimly lit, empty stages. Even so, these empty stages (houses) have a tale to tell (sign on cusp) and it is elsewhere we must look to find the star who owns this part of the theatre (planet ruling sign on cusp) if we are to derive the nature of the tale in question.

On some evenings there is a lull in the proceedings, everyone forgets their lines and fluffs their words; all of the cast are aware of the presence of the actor dressed up as Saturn, though they know that he is really playing a game with them, a game called reality. The stage that this impersonator occupies is a little austere and has a serious background of props. The others tend to avoid this stage but only because they sense a few of their own anxieties in this area—it's not fair that they should blame him for the way he is. The wiser members of the cast sense that Saturn is merely trying to fool them with his disguises; they are deeply aware that the reality he sells them is the one of their own creation, but they are blind enough to buy it anyway.

Between a certain stage and the next there is a glass partition that divides the whole circular stage into half and even another one about three stages forward which splits it even further into four segments. The director has assured us though that there are no real dividing lines between one stage and the next, so that we can proceed from one scene to another, gradually merging the two stories.

The signs will jump from one meaning to another when adjacent; the houses tend to merge gradually leaving traces of the previous house association, depending on how near to the cusp of the next house the planet is. To make it clearer, if one has the Sun placed in the second house using the equal system, it may appear in the third house by using a different system of houses, Koch, Placidus or Porphyry for example. Then, one can even experience the effects of that planet occurring in both houses, though of course, not simultaneously. I once had a client with Saturn in the 3rd (by Koch), but it was placed in the 4th when using equal house and he experienced its effects in either house at different times. To him with Saturn in the 3rd it meant rigid, controlled thinking and when it affected the 4th house it symbolized (not caused) a certain degree of emotional insecurity and withdrawnness.

Ladies and Gentlemen, I present to you, the Astrological Theatre of Houses:

The First House (Rising Sign/Persona): The need for relating to the environment by development of the 'mask that I show to the world'

One must present a fairly acceptable mask to the outside world and this is the face which one presents to strangers, acquaintances and people whom one meets for the first time. On an inner level it is the urge to relate to external conditions and thereby bridge the gap between the subjective scenery and outer reality. The physical objects in the outer world are a focus for these inner projections; it's all in the mind really!

Inner meaning	*Projected onto*
Spontaneous energies of psyche	'Coming across' to others
Urge to put energies out into the world	The way one relates to the public
Symbolic new beginnings	Conditions at actual birth
Urge to define oneself	Physical appearance, mannerisms. The way others see you

The Second House: The urge to make an external object part of myself and so 'possess it'

The first house is a fairly straightforward affair where one attempts to define personality; subordinate to the actual 'being' of oneself are those things which support oneself. In the world around us this means food, shelter, money and the acquisition of material items. The second house then is a process of attaching onself to physical things in order that they may provide a means of security. On this level it represents the things one values or makes special in the concrete world. In this respect it is the person's self-worth or how much he

values what he is, therefore what he thinks he 'owns' or 'possesses'
about himself. Inevitably these possessions appear 'outside' of him—
in the world around him.

Inner meaning	*Projected onto*
The urge to extend oneself over the physical world, making it part of oneself	What you think belongs to you, possessive qualities
The process of attaching oneself to materialism	Money, possessions, luxury items
The urge to support the needs of the physical vehicle	Material security, valuing of one's possessions
The urge to 'possess' something about oneself	Values of self-worth, values of physical attributes

*The Third House: The need to obtain vital information about the
environment and communicate myself by whatever means available*

At this stage both inner and outer meanings of the houses are fairly
accessible, the third house portrays man's need to acquire information
about the environment so that he can function at an adequate level.
It is a process of learning, then, distilling the given data, programming
it and allowing the details to be recalled whenever necessary. It
represents two aspects of the conscious mind process (see Mercury,
Chapter 4) and these mechanisms are focused onto an outer reality
that encompasses them.

Take for instance the processes of communication and learning.
Certain information must be obtained before there is anything to
be communicated at all; even one's inner thoughts have to be recalled
to the conscious mind before one is aware of them. By distributing
this information and receiving feedback from others, one may
perpetuate the process of learning certain facts or providing others
with knowledge. Inevitably, communication will involve moving
around from one place to another in one's everyday world, whether
in one's mind (reading, thinking, watching TV) or in one's
environment. The third house is an inner world and we project it
onto those people whom we meet in our usual, day-to-day comings
and goings, hence the connection with neighbours and brothers and
sisters (our closest neighbours).

Inner meaning	*Projected onto*
Urge to learn, acquire knowledge	School, books, libraries
Need to assimilate facts and express them to others	How you learn, think and talk, conversational abilities
Need to distribute information and acquire more	Public transport, short journeys, the neighbourhood, newspapers, TV/radio

The Fourth House: The need for emotional security on an unconscious level and for whatever will provide it

With the introduction of the Watery houses we have links with the world of Jungian unconsciousness. The fourth house is interchangeable (with the twelfth) as either the personal or collective unconscious world and I am happier with it in its context as the former. The personal unconscious represents the total sum of all experiences acquired in this lifetime, from the moment of birth to the time when we shuffle off the mortal coil. Thus it is an underground basement into which one's deepest personal feelings are poured. Like the fourth house, the personal unconscious is a base on which one can build, deriving a feeling of safety and shelter, somewhere to 'belong to' so one can feel that one is all right with the world.

This support must come from somewhere and it is for this reason that the fourth house has more recently been attributed to projections onto the father, as opposed to the mother. Of course there is no way of separating the two ends of the axis in the same way that parents split up; it depends on which parent provided the background support (fourth) and which one spent most time instilling discipline and authority (tenth) which in this day and age are the roles played by father and mother respectively.

It does not matter that the Moon is connected with the fourth house and therefore the mother; what seems to be in evidence is the structure on which the fourth house symbolism is based, and all structured systems must be inevitably Saturnian. Symbolically, the fourth house appears at the 'foot' of the chart as if it were holding up and supporting the rest of the wheel, a foundation on which everything else is built.

Inner meaning	*Projected onto*
Need for emotional security, support system and place of belonging	Domestic affairs, one's place of residence, usually one's father
Inner landscapes, unconscious need to 'belong'	How you make yourself at home, houses, land, buildings
Need to build inner base	One's private life

The Fifth House: The need to express my ego and re-create part of my 'specialness'

Having secured an emotional foundation on which to build, the need to express oneself in all one's glory makes a follow-up to the fourth house. Underneath the outer effects is the urge not to create, but re-create, aspects of onself that allow ego energies to become manifest in the world. To the cynic, this house could well be labelled 'trivial pursuits' for it involves pastimes pursued for their own sake, that is without any ulterior aim.

In contrast to the first house where one is spontaneously reacting to others and expressing oneself, the fifth house involves an automatic reflection back onto the self; there is the need to re-create part of one's individuality, 'specialness', and present it back to the self or others in order to affirm the identity of the ego. These issues are more personal to the individual in the fifth because the subject is not as concerned with relating to others, which is the primary function of the first–seventh axis.

Inevitably others become involved when the person has not learnt to respect and appreciate himself; then the need arises for the attentions of others. Thus the fifth house often precipitates the need to be loved by others, in many cases the childish desire for attention or compliments which boost the ego. If one cannot get a perspective on one's sense of 'specialness' as a human being, then the demand for love from others becomes paramount.

Inner meaning	*Projected onto*
Urge to express one's uniqueness	Creativity, art, music, entertainment

Urge to re-create aspects of oneself in the physical world	Children, love affairs
Need to pursue things for their own sake	Pastimes, how you have fun, gambling, speculation, pleasure
Need to recognize one's uniqueness	Self-admiration or wanting to be loved by another

The Sixth House: The urge to assemble facts about the environment and gain mastery of the physical world in it

The pleasurable affairs of the fifth house are put to work in the domain of the sixth house; one projects the inner need to maintain the real world onto a host of suitable objects like work, servants, health and food. It is easy to see the common thread running through all of these items when you consider that to adapt to the demands of the physical world, some effort is needed to supply oneself with the goods.

The third house has a thin link with the sixth in one's efforts to adapt to the everyday, normal routine. Everyone makes up their own little routine of communication during the daytime but it is the effort used to put these things in operation that is truly sixth house. The obvious utilitarian notion is that someone will get up in the morning, usually go out to work, return for dinner (perhaps to a wife and two children) and either spend the evening at home relaxing or go out later to socialize, making sure that one returns by a particular hour in order to be able to rise early enough the next morning. All very bourgeois indeed, and the little duties and necessities that appear in between come under the heading of the sixth house.

Inner meaning	*Projected onto*
Need to maintain oneself through effort in physical terms	Work, duty, necessity, health, food
Attitude to maintenance of the material world	Subordinates, servants, anyone working in a lesser capacity than yourself

*The Seventh House: The unconscious desire to seek my compli-
mentary 'other half' through dissolution of the ego*

A so-called unconscious area of the chart that compensates for the
ego-oriented first house and the qualities contained therein. Here
is where we can see the effects of the psyche's motivation towards
harmony and balance, when we come face to face with parts of our
personality—in others. This is only when we have been unaware of
such qualities, however, for most of us this is extremely common.

Fundamentally, it is the house of 'true' relating, that is, being
able to give (of oneself) without sacrificing one's individuality; or
being able to take without demands or burdening one's partner with
too many expectations. Thus, it is the principle of sharing, where
both people can receive mutual benefit from a relationship, neither
one gaining at the expense of the other.

The psyche carries out its natural function to compensate for ego
attributes (1st house) through attracting to it qualities in other
individuals (7th house), who can in some way act as a complimentary
other half.

Inner meaning	*Projected onto*
Psyche's urge to maintain equilibrium	Qualities we invoke in others (projection)
Unconscious need to relate, become whole	Social life, public relations, one-to-one relationships, marriage partner

*The Eighth House: The need for transformation of the ego through
emotional involvement with another*

The second of the 'hidden' houses and therefore one operating below
the levels of consciousness, whereas the seventh is easily made available
through contact with others, the Watery houses represent deep,
hidden aspects of the psyche that do not lend themselves easily to
the conscious mind. Thus we have such abstractions as transformation,
ego-death, crises and drastic change to describe a simple process via
a complex set of descriptions. They are not easily described because
they are not easily met within waking life; the fundamental process
of the eighth though is self-transformation.

This process can only occur when there is a drastic change in
consciousness sufficient enough to alter the existing conditions

around oneself. Self-transcendence can be achieved in merging with others on a deep level. This is why the eighth house is associated with sex and death, though it is often taken to mean actual physical death. It is a psychological death that permeates the frontiers of the eighth, any crisis period invokes great, irrevocable changes whereby some part of the individual 'dies' so that new life can grow in its place. Even the orgasm, in French, is called *le petit mort*—the 'little death'.

The eighth house polarity with the second house is based on the axis of internal-external values. The second house encompasses the need to build a secure wall around itself with what it values most, whereas the eighth needs to destroy aspects of the self by merging with another, but renewing life at the same time. This aspect of merging finds its way into material terms expressed as the desire to join one's resources with another for mutual benefit; hence business mergers, joint bank accounts and insurance policies, the emphasis shifting from mine, to ours.

Inner meaning	*Projected onto*
Need for growth, self-transformation, change	Irrevocable change brought about by crisis
Urge to merge deeply with another	Sex, emotional bondage, business mergers, joint resources
Attunement to death-rebirth cycle in nature	Outer results of another's death: wills, legacies, taxes, insurance

The Ninth House: Urge to expand everyday consciousness and limitations of thought

The transformative processes at work in the eighth have now become raised to loftier levels in this, the last of the Fiery houses. How exactly does one gain a perspective on life? The ninth house is that of the seeker; man has left behind his emotional commitments and needs his own philosophy of the world and for this reason many ninth-housers turn to politics, law, philosophy or religion. In this house, we are looking for the broad spectrum in order to gain the bird's-eye philosophical view, attempting to be our own gurus and teachers. The mysteries of nature may be penetrated in the eighth but they are brought out into the open and speculated upon in the ninth, in order to encompass society as a whole. Any experience that broadens your understanding of the fundamental issues of nature is ninth house, whereas its opposite house is concerned with the facts for their own sake.

The third house encompasses short journeys as a means of communication to function effectively in the environment. The ninth house widens that field because new experiences are sought to broaden one's horizons, hence it is projected on long-distance travel, abroad, foreign cultures, further education, etc.

Inner meaning	*Projected onto*
Urge towards expansion of everyday consciousness	Higher education, universities, philosophy, religion, spiritual matters, eastern mysticism
Identification with 'universal mind'	God image, places of worship
Need to expand awareness in general, transcend limitations of environment	Foreign travel, foreign people, cult religions, matters abroad, a spiritual guru/teacher

The Tenth House: Urge for ego-identification with the social order in terms of personal achievement

We return here to the authority figures of our childhood, the things shaping us into a functional, workable being. All of our ideas of being moulded into society's frame have been born out of the relationship with the tenth house. As adults it is the area with which we identify in terms of personal achievement and recognition. Strong tenth-housers feel the need to accomplish something worthwhile 'out there' for themselves as an ambition, whereas the ninth house may be happy merely philosophizing.

For many, the authority figure in childhood is the mother, as she is usually the parent who has spent the most time with the child during infancy, the one who said 'No, you mustn't do that'. If for an individual then, the fourth house means 'father', then the tenth house energies are projected onto the mother.

Much of this early conditioning is geared towards helping the child function later in life in society, and 'make his mark in the world'. The individual will eventually want to establish something that bears the mark of his identity, not unlike the fifth house. The difference is that the tenth house has a larger goal to accomplish, some end in sight whereas the fifth is pursued for its own sake. Thus the tenth house represents your ultimate aims in the material world, ambitions, goals and objectives and also includes those who are 'further up the ladder' and will at some time appear in a more powerful or authoritative position than yourself.

Inner meaning	*Projected onto*
Identification with 'mother image' (as a rule), conditions, laws imposed from within.	Bosses, employers, officialdom in general, laws imposed from without
Ego-identification with larger social order as highest level of functioning in material terms	Goals, ambitions, one's public image, career, profession, role in society, status symbols, reputation

The Eleventh House: The need for group identification and the values of the collective

The eleventh house is concerned with matters on a collective level that strips away the personal achievements of the tenth, and makes them the concerns of the group. What is good for the group, as opposed to what is good for me and mine. Underneath this attitude you may detect a type of dogmatism, because once you are a member of that group, there is the same set of rules and regulations as existing in the tenth house experience. From an individual point of view, it represents man's urge to identify himself with the collective, to contribute part of himself to the needs and aspirations of the group as a whole. Teamwork makes it possible to achieve things much easier for the rest of humanity by pulling together common goals and wishes; thus many eleventh-housers perform work for the community, offer their services to charity or belong to local clubs and societies that share a common aim. Friends also appear under this heading, but only when they are part of a larger unit to which one belongs such as meeting places, and social gatherings. I feel that 'best friends' or 'bosom pals' come under the seventh house because they imply more intimate types of relationship.

Polarized with the fifth, the eleventh house is a sharing group-consciousness house that is to do with ego of the collective whereas the fifth needs ego-identity for itself but needs others for it to be recognized. This, however, is not intrinsically a fundamental issue. The fifth house does not need others to recognize its creativity when it has assured itself of its own identity. The eleventh house has no such identity of its own and needs to form a team into which individual energies are pooled.

Inner meaning	Projected onto
Urge towards 'group consciousness'	Humanitarian issues, 'causes'
Denigration of ego-self in favour of group ego	Clubs, societies, the community, concern for the future of mankind
Urge to be part of a larger whole	Groups of friends, acquaintances, social gatherings

The Twelfth House: The urge towards dissolution of the ego and the attainment of one-ness

The twelfth is one of the most inaccessible houses to plunder for meaning because the very things it represents are by nature hidden, illusory and tend to slip from view quite easily. The social boundaries and issues of right and wrong existent in the eleventh house are dissipated here, and one thing is not quite so distinct from another. If the eleventh represents the urge for greater social integration, then the twelfth completes the process with the dissolution of all boundaries, attempting to achieve a one-ness with the whole of life itself. The Chinese philosophical system of Taoism requires that man imitates the effortlessness of nature, gracefully moving with the ebb and flow of change. This is part of the inner urge of the twelfth, to become one with nature. Inevitably it requires the giving up of one's ego, the sacrifice to something greater than oneself and a realization of the awesome power of life's processes that disregard mere individuals like us. Nature often seems cruel and heartless when we are faced with the inevitable, death.

The collective unconscious is a vault containing the whole of man's psychic history, i.e. the conditioning of his mind from the time he began to think and act in various ways, which we have inherited as the brain becomes more and more sophisticated. These associations open up a whole cartload of Jungian connections; the Shadow, personal unconscious and the archetypes associated with the collective unconscious. The twelfth house as the Shadow is portrayed in the way in which we are apt to repress an extraordinary showcase of undesirable emotions, 'evil' thoughts and unlived-out energies as if it were some kind of private garbage bag, the dustbin of the astrological houses.

These energies are rendered undesirable in favour of the ego and become shut away, behind the first house. Therefore they are energies that we have lost contact with, being so much out of favour with the lonely ego. The emotional experiences acquired in this life are part of the personal unconscious, and the Shadow forms part of it, so there is a link with this and the twelfth house although I would chiefly consider it under the collective tag. They are further interchangeable because the collective unconscious is to do with one's hereditary roots, which links it with the fourth house.

Now for the astrology. The key urge with the twelfth house is that of dissolution and the breaking down of all barriers that separate us from others on a feeling level. Whereas the eighth house was an intimate feeling link with another individual, the twelfth house is a kind of intimacy with nature herself, God, the great being, one-ness or whatever you prefer to call it. Because planets in the twelfth house tend to become dissipated in their energies, they do not act as fully conscious energies, that is we often do not feel them quite so strongly. Nevertheless they do not act weakly in the life of an individual since much of the energy is projected, and we know how powerful projections can be. It is as if the energy is denied its true expression, so either the individual receives a blow of fate on the head (via unconscious projection) or he puts those energies to use in a way that is non-egoistic or for the good of others.

Many positive twelfth-housers use the feeling undercurrents in a passive way (if you can call it that) and retire from the outside world to contemplate their innermost self. Many will pursue meditation, clairvoyance, visualization or yoga. All of these practices will require a state of non-self, passivity and quiet contemplation. Other twelfth-housers deny themselves freedom in some way and use twelfth-house energy to relieve the suffering of others, working in hospitals, the caring professions and practices that deny personal gain. In this case, the Shadow energy is projected onto an actual outside object. Remember the twelfth-house undesirable, repressed, so-called evil contents? Places of confinement in our society house the people we have either considered physically ill (hospitals), mentally ill (mental institutions) or evil, therefore a threat to others (prisons). The energies of the twelfth house are not neutralized by repression, so the psyche projects them onto other people, making us our own worst enemy.

On a personal front, people with twelfth house planets often express this urge to 'dissolve' as it were, by escaping everyday reality, in a variety of ways. The simple act of seeking solitude and shutting oneself from others for a while allows them their own reality experience, a private dreamworld and fantasy land, because too much reality is hard to cope with. That inner world can be heightened by alcohol or drugs, anything to prolong the ecstasy of escape.

This feeling of living in another world while they're well and truly here and now, may only be described by the person with a strong twelfth house himself, a feeling that he's cut off from the rest of us. This is one of the reasons why they do not assert themselves very strongly, and are apt to be rather shy and retiring. Perhaps they've found God after all.

Inner meaning	*Projected onto*
Inner urge to dissolve all boundaries of consciousness	Escapism, drugs, alcohol, meditation, spiritualism, yoga, etc.
Unconscious 'shadowy' energies seeking identification	Prisons, hospitals, places of confinement, victims, secret enemies
Expression of non-egoistic energies	Compassion, service to the sick and needy

Zodiac Personas—a Light-Hearted Look at the Sign on the Ascendant

Aries ♈

When one is running head down with horns pointed at target, it is difficult to see precisely where one is going. Urgency and immediacy prevail as the chief characteristics of this ascendant. Aries rising is impatient, from the tip of his reddish hair to the ends of his hurried feet, striking you as someone with a million and one things to do; he probably has. Advise him not to scatter his energies too much if he really wants to accomplish something worthwhile. He is not likely to listen though—he has to be in charge. 'At least we're getting a bit of excitement at last,' says Aries rising as you study the clear baby-faced complexion, then, he's off again to fight more black knights on his trusty steed before you can say Libra on the descendant.

Aries rising has a secret soul that yearns for a real partnership, the give and take variety, but this is the unconscious half of him.

Oh how he would love to be able to relax into a peaceful relationship as a counterbalance to his activities in the jousting tournaments. Who would have guessed? Who else but the princess?

Taurus ♉

Taurus rising is, to say the least, motivated somewhat by material concerns. Having noticed the graceful swan-like neck or conversely, a heavy, squat neck, you can observe them installed in their little semi-detached, tucking into a box of chocolates after they've managed to force down most of their favourite meal. Well, they are just a little fond of luxury; that goes for your body too if you happen to go out with one of them. Anything that stimulates their fondness for touch is A.1 with Taurus rising. Tasteful clothes, the smell of your hair, the rustling of notes and coins, the whiff of their favourite delicacy and of course, your arm around them—all sheer poetry to this rising sign.

Scorpio falls on the descendant so that Taurus rising houses a deeper emotional current than is at first observed; both signs strive for security but the unconscious half here buries deeper in an almost self-destructive fashion to penetrate the underside of relationships. What? Stable, placid Taurus rising? Beneath the earthy exterior there is a longing to delve into the unknown watery depths of life; if only they could realize that the depths belong to them too in their relationships.

Gemini ♊

Gemini rising is often easily spotted. If you happen to enter a crowded room just follow your ears; he's the one talking everyone to death, making them laugh with acute comic timing and witty asides. Then he'll switch to a serious monotone on any subject you care to mention with the verbal dexterity of a politician. There is an alive, twinkling look in the eyes and in more ways than one.

Gemini rising natives are typical eggheads. Firstly, they are students *per se*. Not only do they enjoy learning at school but they are pupils who attend the school of life in general; curious, intelligent and eager for knowledge about almost everything. The other reference to eggs is their oval-shaped face with fresh, youthful looks that can remain up until the age of 50. In conversation with them you will never be bored, especially if they perform their usual habit of changing sides when cornered by a tricky question.

At the root of Gemini rising is the inner man who wants to fit the jigsaw puzzle of knowledge together in order to gain a richer understanding of the meanings of life. Sagittarius on the seventh may look to others for a spiritual teacher, never recognizing that he is his own guru.

Cancer ♋

There is something of the typical moon face about Cancer rising, they look like pale little tin-men from outer space. They're quite fond of their stomachs too. That's where all those moody cravings go when they're depressed; then they eat, eat, eat. Cancer rising wears its feelings on its sleeve and is not averse to shedding the odd tear at a sentimental, touching moment. Their eyes water and the tears roll down those pale, translucent cheeks of theirs.

One of the main features of Cancer rising is its changeable moods, observable clinginess and their eagerness to feed house visitors tea and scones at the drop of a hat. They're mothers to the world but not much fun if you're on a diet.

Beneath the emotionalism, there is Capricorn on the seventh house cusp, here is where they find their own built in self-sufficiency, pragmatism and ability to strive against difficult odds. I wonder if they ever do find it, though.

Leo ♌

Leo rising proudly projects itself to others with rampant, feline individuality, and a great many of them look like pussy cats if you inspect the eyes closely. An abundant, rich crop of hair is something else to look for, good colouring and a noble air; all are characteristic of the Leo persona. Their outward regal mannerisms seldom betray the unconscious Aquarius seventh house, that identifies with group equality and collective rights. 'The man off the street has no right to impinge upon me and myself', says Leo rising. Lesser mortals will notice that this rising sign needs to be centre stage but cannot thrive without the appraisals of others. The good points are their endearing honesty, chivalry and sunny disposition, even this is painted with just a dash of arrogance. Out of my way, peasant.

Drawing the seventh house Aquarius onto itself as it does, Leo ascendants need to relate to the 'average' person without thinking that they're either better or worse off than him. But their rising sign won't let them.

Virgo ♍

Good old clean, neat and tidy Virgo rising is the well-mannered and polite figure in the corner at the friend's meeting when you are discussing the politics of business management in the twentieth century. Note the slight, athletic, even nervous figure (though they don't twitch as much as Gemini) who looks as if he couldn't even raise one eyebrow let alone keep to a tight schedule in the boardroom. Don't be fooled, this guy has bags of energy, a tick-tock brain that can juggle several thousand details around at once and the ability to sort out any kind of mess you care to mention. You will also have observed that Virgo rising may not participate much verbally, but how appropriately dressed he is, what taste, what style. As long as he satisfies himself that he's done a job worth doing and done it well, creating an impression is of secondary importance.

With Pisces on the seventh house cusp, the unconscious side of him longs to let go to a partner and have his hair let down, so to speak. He yearns to give his all, emotionally, and let those old feelings flow. After all, it's hard work behind a typewriter all day.

Libra ♎

Now here's a graduate from the charm school; sweet, kind, charming Libra rising is the antithesis of selfish old Aries rising. They love talking to people; not only do they overflow with grace and style themselves but they are masters of the art of getting the best out of *you*. Bringing out the best in someone creates a pleasant atmosphere for one and all; they can be as interesting to listen to as they are good at listening. Yes, they've learned the secret of popularity.

The women are painted dolls and the men are almost too good-looking. They both radiate Venusian charm and play it to the hilt. Who can resist them? You wouldn't dream of burdening them with your black moods or pent-up frustrations; you'd feel so uncivilized and inferior. Anyway you're in company now so wait until you get home to pick your teeth.

With the Aries seventh house underside, there is an unconscious selfishness that may show in the need for manipulation and desire to win. Needless, to say, it's all done in the best *possible taste*. Selfish? Libra rising? Heaven forbid.

Scorpio ♏

Not all Scorpio risings look like Count Dracula you know, but they do give themselves away by trying to hide too much. They simply cannot contain all of that intense energy; they need to lift the kettle lid now and then to give off some steam—though not in public you understand. This is Scorpio rising's need to maintain control over themselves. Life is often a battlefield to them but the war is being fought internally. Observe the piercing eyes, heavy eyebrows and steady gaze; hear the cutting truth, stinging sarcasm (only when you've upset them or they can't relate to a situation) and watch how they react when you ask a personal question. Well, it's your fault for asking, you should have known that Scorpio rising likes its little secrets, bless 'em. Most of their actions are so designed as not to reveal too much about themselves; the way they talk, walk, look and reply to your nosey questions.

With Taurus on the descendant there is something in them that yearns for peace and tranquillity in a secure relationship. This penetrative and often destructive rising sign belies their unconscious side. In fact, they're pretty simple and boring at heart.

Sagittarius ♐

Not to be overlooked this one; candid, optimistic and outspoken are the Sagittarius risings. If you've ever wondered why the crazy character with the horse's chin always greets you with a smile at the bus stop every morning you can rest assured that it's not from any devious motive. He is as open and honest as a day is long—surely you remember him telling you that your false teeth make you look like an attractive mortician. He's being truthful of course. Malicious? Never. In any case, poking fun is sometimes a cure-all for the starched shirts who haven't learned how to laugh at life. Sagittarius rising sees the broad view, the big picture, it's just the finer nuances that he misses. Humour is his forte, for this is another one of his expansive and carefree attitudes to things; he will tell you exactly what is on his mind, it's up to you whether or not you can stand it.

Gemini falls on the seventh house cusp, with an unconscious need to fit those details into the picture he has already envisioned. In relationships they need someone to keep their feet on the ground with the here and now facts. At least they can talk each other to death.

Capricorn ♑

Capricorn rising looks out upon this world with dark, serious, often mistrustful eyes. Note the cautious, even timid approach of Capricorn rising who seems too serious for his own good. This ascendant has the look of a slightly older and wiser schoolteacher who waits patiently to correct your every mistake. As the years roll on he doesn't seem to age quite as fast as you do and there's the added bonus of his dry, sardonic wit. He wants to present a self-sufficient, capable image to the rest of the world so he immerses himself in the practical running of his life which is just as much of a job to him as his nine-to-five stint at the office. Outwardly he's shy and self-conscious, inwardly he's a hero, a romantic, but his rising sign's got its foot in the door.

Cancer on the descendant makes him yearn for the soft life; someone to warm his slippers after a hard day's grind is what he needs. This 'mumsy' side of Capricorn rising is seldom noticed, especially by himself. Just ask his wife.

Aquarius ♒

Aquarius rising just has to be different, especially in the way they present themselves. Dress is unimportant as long as it's unconventional. It's called style, brother. Hip? Cool? Call them what you will; conservative they're not. Look for a taller build than most and a faraway look to the eyes; this is when you catch them thinking deeply about the mysteries of life on other planets, as if there wasn't enough of it here! They'll often present themselves as a friend and confidante; they can converse with anyone from the hippy to the stuffed shirt business executive; everybody's the same underneath, man, and he's waiting for you to realize it too. To hell with society, convention and normality, you don't make much impact that way; don't you want to be a real, honest person instead of a cardboard cut-out of the establishment?

Leo on the seventh plays a very different role so that unconsciously, Aquarius rising is fairly conservative and seeks 'normal' people with 'normal' egos. Why are their partners so bossy and full of themselves?

Pisces ♓

Fish faces rule OK? Well, only if you happen to have a Pisces ascendant; everyone else smirks and titters about the flat feet, droopy arms and face like a conger eel. These Neptunian peepers are you must admit, quite beautiful; deep, languid pools that you could quite easily drown in. All of their sensitivities show up on that face you know, right down to the shy, timid expressions that make you want to drop whatever you're doing and help them out. Pisces rising looks out upon this world with eyes full of compassion; they can't resist a sob story in fact. They have plenty of their own to tell but at least they'll listen first. The complexion is usually pale, almost translucent, but there are many shapes and sizes, just as there are different types of fish.

If there is one minute failing with them, it's their lack of assertion and direction—they really need to dig their heels in more. Then, you have the most sympathetic, warm and tolerant rising sign of them all, with the courage to forge ahead to match.

Virgo on the descendant houses the realistic and efficient side that they need to bring out. Is it really the partner who is too materialistic and pedantic?

6.
DYNAMICS OF PSYCHIC ENERGY— THE ASPECTS

Aspects are measurements of degrees on the zodiac that allow planets at the same degree to link with one another. Planets at 9° Scorpio and 9° Taurus are in opposition to each other because they are in opposite signs. (For further information, see Appendix II.)

Aspects provide either an easy or difficult blend of the two planets' natures and it is the major ones, conjunctions, sextile, square, trine, quincunx and opposition, which concern us here. Some parts of our nature do not blend so easily with others and the so-called hard aspects (conjunction, square, quincunx and opposition) have a lot to answer for when exacerbating tensions and struggles appear to get the better of us. Even worse, others come along to disrupt our lives just when we thought all was going well. It's hard sometimes when you can't seem to pull it all together, suffering from inner niggles and compulsions with all the countenance of a famished tiger who has just decided it's time for a dinner. But where's the food? What's stopping you from getting exactly what you want? Why the obstacles?

Wherever there is tension, there is friction, and the by-product is energy. What happens to the sulphur at the end of a matchstick when it is struck? Jung used the term 'libido' to denote the energy produced by the psyche as a result of direct experience with life, on an inner or outer level. It is up to an individual then to determine exactly how this potential energy will be expressed through the birth chart and its symbols. Aspects then provide channels via their joining together of planets, for a particular mode of expression peculiar to those two planets.

The 'hard' aspects produce more of this energy than do the 'easy' aspects since it is common for human beings to resist strong affects— anger, hate, evil-mindedness, etc.—and thereby create the tension within themselves. When there is no such resistance there seems to be a natural flow of libido, seemingly with a life all of its own. Squares seem to create a major difficulty for everyone. This is because there are two different kinds of motivation, each one unsympathetic to the other. Inevitably, squares build up inner friction and tension and we are apt to cut ourselves off from vital energies that need very much to be expressed. Also, any aspect can be the subject of projection when we deny part of our own nature the room to be acknowledged and released. Here are the major aspects:

The Hard Angles—Conjunction, Square, Quincunx and Opposition

These are often the ones that make us get up on our feet and *do* something, especially when the situation has become so stale that there's nothing left to do except change the record. The situation will probably beat you to it though. The conjunction is, at best, a focusing of those two planets on a specific area in life which provides depth, concentration and hopefully, understanding. At worst, this concentration of energy closes off other areas of life almost as if they didn't exist, like when your lover says, 'Oh, but I don't even want to *know* that'. And you sit and think, 'How ignorant can you get?'

A planet conjunct an angle is intense because all of that planet's energy is heaped out there all at once. One is acutely aware of that type of energy affecting the house that follows the particular angle; they are much more obvious facets of one's personality, when planets come within 8° of any of the four angles. They are most noticeable conjunct the Ascendant or MC, that is, to the public at large. The people at home of course, notice the ones on the IC and Descendant.

Aspects are like any of those adult puzzles where you have to find your way to the centre of a labyrinth, tracing your pencil from either of the four corners to try to reach the centre, until you come up against another wall. Then you have to find another way through the maze, some passages are blocked and are easy to see, some are thoroughfares that appear open until you turn a corner and bump your head into yet another sealed-off entrance.

Likewise, some planets aspect each other with remarkable grace and smoothness, allowing a soft ride for the energies to come out. Two more planets will resist each other, rather like the walls within the maze resisted your attempts to freewheel through its passageways. If there is no link provided, then obviously one is cut off and either left stranded or forced to go in another direction. Aspects are such links within the birth chart: a rich tapestry which blends some elements and makes a mockery of others. Planets placed in the same element blend quite naturally, as do planets located in sympathetic elements—remember the auxiliary functions? Thus planets in Fire will get on well with planets in Air; unfortunately Fire (in astrology) is incompatible with Water (unlike the types) and, as you can imagine, abhorrent to Earth.

What is not so pleasing then, are planets in such noxious relationships as Fire and Water or Fire and Earth; with the first combination we have elements of signs which are in square to each other but still possess the same attitude. For instance, Aries and Cancer are signs separated by ninety degrees. Both are intent on running the show but their energies are directed towards different ends, hence they clash with one another.

Taurus and Leo are another two signs in square to each other, both are stubborn and opinionated but fix their sights on completely different goals. Gemini and Virgo repeats the same theme; both are versatile and adaptable but for quite different reasons.

The square therefore is a challenge that says, 'What are you going to actually *do* with these two planets?' There's no real way in which they can operate harmoniously, each one resisting the other, so that a tension arises when they simply won't play ball with each other, which as you can imagine, happens quite often. Then it can become part of a projected energy, and let's make one thing clear: any aspect of psychic energy that cannot be integrated into the conscious life will become projected onto a suitable object. That includes all of the aspects, not just the opposition, which is something that astrologers often fail to point out. At best, the friction arising from a square produces self-motivation, the acceptance of the challenge and a willing of those energies into a variety of productive channels. At worst it is counter-productive and leaves one feeling thwarted by life's obstacles, generating a feeling of being cut off in some way.

As mentioned earlier, the opposition is often described in connection with one's unconscious projections to others because of its first–seventh house connotation. This implies that one end of the opposition is dispensed with and foisted onto the partner. Textbooks are often at pains to point out its effects in relationships, the qualities we invoke in others and the conflict arising from disagreements and opposite points of view. It appears that the opposition is more accessible and therefore more readily dealt with than the square, which tends to produce more of an internal battle. The difficulties are created through non-awareness of this mechanism when: 'It's always their fault!'; 'How dare he treat me that way when I was so kind to him!'; or 'Why are they always so argumentative?'

These declarations can be heard when stuck in one end of the opposition. If the aspect occurs between a personal planet and an outer one, you can guess which end of the opposition is projected. With Saturn it is always the mysterious 'they' who are trying, cold-hearted, cynical and dogmatic. One's personal planets in opposition to Uranus draws the individual to the safe end of the scale so that it is the partner who cannot buckle down, is always leaving, never shows warmth or is unpredictable. When Neptune is projected, the 'other one' is criticized for his indecisiveness, lack of direction, daydreaming and alcoholism. Pluto is also a burden and a personal planet in opposition to it draws qualities from the partner that are threatening, obsessive, demanding and then one feels in danger of being completely drained of life blood, as if something is out to get you.

The function of the opposition is to raise awareness of self through others, but this is only done with a good, long hard look at ourselves. You will be able to say, of course, that any aspect is indicative of this, until we arrive at the quincunx. This aspect is like a bolt from the blue and stands apart from the square and opposition like an unwelcome relative turning up at your daughter's wedding. If one can roughly define the square as internal tension, resistance and blockedness, the opposition as polarity, projection and awareness of others, then the quincunx can encompass all of these, and more.

Put into a better perspective it often produces niggles and tensions that are basically trivial, but seldom fail to make your blood pressure rise to abnormal limits. You've just no idea why God decided to punish you today as you miss the bus, spill your dinner in the restaurant, run out of change for the gas meter or forget to cancel the milk when you go on holiday. These are representative of the exasperating tensions produced by the quincunx. The two planets making this aspect are unsympathetic by polarity, element and quadruplicity. That is, one planet in a masculine sign, the other in a feminine; one planet say, in a Water sign, the other in an Air sign; one planet in a Cardinal sign and the other in a Fixed sign. The two I am thinking of here are Cancer and Aquarius; imagine how radically different these two signs are. With planets in quincunx to one another, the only possible thing that can happen is for things to blow up in your face, or go off like a damp squib.

Situations arising in the environment from a quincunx are often unexpected and sudden. There is nothing one can do to bring about a change in this situation; it requires that you let go and give in to it. The clash has already taken place at a psychological level and soon finds its way into the real world, as a sudden event. It tests your reactions to this outer occurrence and therefore measures how much you think you may have to give up, how much you need to let go of. Is it really the end of the world because the dog's chewed the carpet again?

The Soft Aspects—the Sextile and the Trine

I hope by now that there is at least some difference in your definition of the aforementioned 'malefic' aspects. As far as I am concerned, the separating factor between the benefic sextile and trine is very small indeed. Both planets are placed in elements which contact one another agreeably and so their effects are often difficult to observe. Imagine I am travelling down a motorway at an average speed of 60 mph, with the cars behind and in front of me likewise driving at the same speed, each a safe distance from the car ahead. One could almost fall asleep. In fact when I observe the vehicle in front, it hardly feels as if I am moving at all. Well, that's how it is with trines and sextiles. Things can flow along and you don't even notice they're moving at all.

The sextile is usually more productive than the trine in terms of production itself—that is, the effort to get things done. With the trine, there is simply no effort needed; you're already good at it, perhaps you pass off your various in-born talents with shrugged shoulders. No matter, others will recognize them and praise you for it. Planets aspecting each other in the same element blend easily, there is a natural flow between the two, like the tyres at 60 mph on the motorway in our previous scenario. The only occasions to produce a negative effect are the ones when you rest at the wheel of the car, passively admiring the view and letting the rest of the world go by. There is nothing intrinsically negative about this of course, except that you never get anything done and this is how trines can make you lazy and unproductive.

When the trine works positively it is a harmonizing, stabilizing influence, allowing the individual to express potential in the sweetest possible way. It is like the relationship of the first house (Fire) to the other Fire houses, the fifth and ninth. The elements blend together almost unnoticed by the individual until he surprises himself saying, 'Well, I never knew I could do that'.

Sextiles are not as potent in their energy content; the libido is operating through elements that have some common ground but it is the effort of the individual, having called upon these energies, that gets things done. Again, there is a smooth interaction once the libido is released, not frustrated as in the square. The sextile also allows one to communicate those two energies easily to others, not necessarily in words, as anyone with a Venus–Pluto sextile will tell you.

7

PAINTING THE PICTURE: JUNGIAN CHART INTERPRETATION

How are we to analyse the chart in the light of Jungian symbols? As in genethliacal (natal chart) astrology, we need a point of departure which gives us a general outline within which to paint the more intricate details; eventually one will have a portrait of the whole person, or at least we hope so. Natal charts break down in the face of personal preference, parental conditioning and factors arising in the environment that can distort the true nature of an individual as the chart unfolds during life. What we can say is what it is possible for an individual to express in one's lifetime, what there is a need to make room for and perhaps how the individual will manifest those energies present according to the situation he is born into.

As a general rule of thumb, one gains the overall background scenery by looking at the balance and imbalance of astrological elements and whether or not they are masculine or feminine energies, which brings us right away to the psychological types:

'Typing' the Chart

Immediately it would seem that counting the number of planets in each element and observing which has most presents no particular problem. Theoretically, a chart full of planets in Fire signs suggests intuition as the main function and an inferior sensation function. Generally this would be the case, but in my experience I have found the system to break down when there are planets conjunct the ascendant and midheaven. The elemental quality of the planets therefore must be taken into consideration:

Fire

The Sun and Mars are pure fire, the former is the solar principle of self and creativity, the latter is the archetype of action, energy and the will to assert. Uranus is part Fiery because of its lightning-like, sudden quality, but belongs more under the Air category.

Earth
Saturn is the only purely Earthy planet, connected with form, structure and materialism.

Air
Mercury is Air personified, as in the Roman god of the same name, hence communication, thinking and travel.

Water
The Moon and Neptune consist only of Water in astrology. The Moon symbolizes feeling responses and the need for emotional security. Neptune is a feeling response that encompasses the ideal or illusory reality. Pluto has some Water in its ability to penetrate deeply, but is Fiery once the explosive nature is expressed. Jupiter perhaps ought to appear under the Fire heading and indeed much of its intrinsic nature is expressed this way. It is also mixed with a little Air and Water, partly (a) because of its philosophical and reflective nature, and partly (b) because it is a protective and supportive planet. Venus is left until last because it is a combination of at least three elements. Water because of its emphasis on feminine responses, Air because of its social and communicate aspects and Earth, since it is fond of materialism and luxury.

Presuming that the individual is expressing the patterns of energy without hindrance, we may proceed to 'type' the chart observing the usual protocol. One determining factor is whether the planets under consideration are personal ones or generational influences. Planets from the Sun to Mars, if many of them occupy one element, will almost certainly point to the superior function and at the same time we have an idea of the function which is weakest in expression, that of the opposite element. If there are personal planets in Fire then one is looking at an intuitive type which makes Earth the weakest function. Then there are the auxiliary functions to consider; the elements that serve that purpose in this case are Air and Water. Intuition can be backed up with thinking and feeling, but never sensation, and already a picture is forming of the basic function of consciousness. Further weight may be added by the inclusion of the ascendant's element; this is vital because the whole of consciousness peers through the ascendant's window. I have found on numerous occasions that this area of the chart points to

either the superior or a strong auxiliary function; very seldom
does it manifest as the weakest.

Looking at the Persona

One's outer physical characteristics are the most obvious facet that
one is presented with on meeting someone for the first time and
as I have mentioned before, the element of the ascendant is often
the same as the main function. The persona is presented as the mask
donned for the purposes of social interaction, and beneath this
exterior there is a subconscious process in operation that acts
automatically to 'protect' the individual. In short, it is a defence
mechanism, activated in order to protect one's inner nature, the
qualities that are 'up front' so to speak.

Your rising sign switches on automatically whenever there is the
subconscious instinct towards self-protection, in order not to be
caught in an unguarded moment. You may have experienced this
inner drama yourself many times. During your so-called 'unguarded
moments' when the drawbridge of consciousness is let down, one
is apt in lots of cases, either to talk or sing to oneself when alone
and sure that no one else is watching or listening. In these moments
we can happily communicate with ourselves because we are free to
say and do what we please; witness our reaction when someone walks
into the room. We cease talking to ourselves to begin with, our
attention has been diverted and we are 'on guard'. If the other person
is not 'close' to you in any way, then your mask slips back immediately
on to your face, the defence mechanism is reactivated and your rising
sign goes into action.

Inevitably, planets placed in the first house or aspecting the
ascendant will give the persona a different colour scheme, according
to the energies they symbolize.

What are you Projecting?

Everything that remains unconscious is projected, so there are no
actual specific areas in which one can look to see which planetary
energies will become a source of projection. Needless to say the
obvious place to begin with is the seventh house and planets
contained therein but there is always the individual to consider. If
the person is attempting to become aware of seventh house planets
and the source of his projections, then he will not feel as much that
his relationships are fated in the way many often do. It is true that
the descendant area of the chart is often an unconscious one, but
what if, say, the Sun is placed there: can one be unconscious of that?

One must tread carefully on the grounds of horoscope delineation, lest one run the risk of over-simplification or at the other end of the scale, over-emphasis on minute details. The Sun placed in the seventh house is weakened, only to the extent that it cannot shine with its usual brightness without the company of others; it finds difficulty living its life alone and brings the best out of itself through interaction with a partner. Therefore it is unconscious in one sense, it is unaware of its own solar power in its own right. Sun seventh-housers may lack that feeling of 'specialness' or self-confidence and the energy is projected onto others who can express their own sunny nature quite easily. It is common for the Sun-seventh house individual to enter the hero-worship syndrome, revering others who possess a strong sense of self, while it is not lived out in themselves.

A difficult planet will be foisted upon someone else in projection where there are hard aspects between inner and outer planets and it must be said that some of these pairs make very disagreeable bedfellows. Consider a hard angle between the Moon and Saturn; consciousness is likely to allow only the Moon enough to breathe, so it is others who are burdensome and restrictive when you are only trying your best to please. How can they be so heartless, cutting you off like that?

Seriously though, such aspects are for want of a better word, trying. Saturn is never easy to deal with wherever he is placed and in conjunction, square and opposition to your personal planets is usually dispensed with via unconscious projection. Look to your own chart and the hard angles and ask yourself whether or not you are blaming others too much for the things that happen to you. Whenever these inner elements are unrecognized and one cannot come to terms with the transpersonal energies of Uranus, Neptune and Pluto, they visit us through others and wreak what seems to be an impossible, irrevocable fate.

But we are our own fates.

The Parents' Axis and the Personal Unconscious
The IC/MC axis denotes the starting post of individual development that culminates in worldly success (or failure) depending on the inherent predisposition of the individual. By the more esoterically inclined, the fourth house has been marked out as both the womb and the tomb, the beginning and the end of life, since we enter the world in much the same way as we leave it. This is nothing to do with the actual means of death; rather, it implies a state of unconsciousness. The fourth house as the beginning of life is another

sound reason to propose that it belongs to the mother, but as experience has shown, this is not always the case. One can gain a fairly clear picture of one's experience of upbringing and parental conditioning using areas related to the fourth–tenth house axis since it denotes one's emotional feeling base and at the opposite pole, one's so-called adult life.

A suitable point of departure is the sign on the cusp of the fourth house, which ought to begin with the IC (I am not over-fond of using the Equal House system, since the IC and MC angles rarely fall at the beginning of the fourth and tenth houses, even though they are the true cusps). The sign on the fourth shows your attitude to domestic matters as a whole, and the sign on the tenth merely compensates, and points to your attitudes to 'making it' and achieving something in the world. It goes without saying that the projections onto the parents will derive from the influences of the Moon and Saturn by their positions on the chart as the so-called ruling planets of the fourth and tenth respectively.

Generally speaking, the fourth house cusp falls three signs away from the Ascendant, a Taurus rising for instance would have Leo on the fourth house cusp and Aquarius therefore at the cusp of the tenth. Taking into consideration the Moon sign and the effect of Saturn, here is a table that will point to the sort of home environment you will have experienced.

Parent's Axis

ARIES (on 4th house cusp)
LIBRA (on 10th)
(Capricorn rising)

Aries on the fourth needs independence to build their own inner base, they just have to be in charge at home. They are superb, charming, manipulators with others whilst getting ahead in life.

TAURUS (on 4th house cusp)
SCORPIO (on 10th)
(Aquarius rising)

Taurus' inner environment needs to be peaceful and serene, perhaps near where there's lots of grass. They forge ahead into the world intent on succeeding through brains and will-power.

GEMINI (on 4th house cusp)
SAGITTARIUS (on 10th)
(Pisces rising)

Gemini on the fourth's carefree attitude towards home gains momentum as they spend more and more time chasing their career. Idealists they are in these areas, slightly irresponsible though!

CANCER (on 4th house cusp)
CAPRICORN (on 10th)
(Aries rising)

Home is where the heart is for these people; it makes a welcome change after battling to be boss all day. Enterprising and intensely ambitious where goals are concerned.

LEO (on 4th house cusp)
AQUARIUS (on 10th)
(Taurus rising)

The maintenance of a regal inner base drives these individuals, often proud of their family heritage. They put their collective ideas into their ambitions to build for a future.

VIRGO (on 4th house cusp)
PISCES (on 10th)
(Gemini rising)

These individuals learned about discrimination and order at home; perhaps one of the parents fussed a lot. They break away from this at the other end of the scales though!

LIBRA (on 4th house cusp)
ARIES (on 10th)
(Cancer rising)

Diplomats at home, the go-between in family feuds, now you wouldn't go upsetting Cancer rising would you? Energetic careerist though.

SCORPIO (on 4th house cusp)
TAURUS (on 10th)
(Leo rising)

These proud individuals don't yield easily to parents, but they remain tied to their roots and never forget what parents taught them. Just as stubborn with other authorities of course.

SAGITTARIUS (on 4th house cusp)
GEMINI (on 10th)
(Virgo rising)

Always missing from home these people, maybe they moved often as children and they fondly remember their upbringing. Varied career interests wouldn't you know, they got those early on too.

CAPRICORN (on 4th house cusp)
CANCER (on 10th)
(Libra rising)

Could these people really have had strict parents? Responsible and serious about home life, sensitive about career matters, often opting for the caring professions.

AQUARIUS (on 4th house cusp)
LEO (on 10th)
(Scorpio rising)

Detachment from parents often necessary here, the demand for freedom is so great. Friends are welcomed anytime. Their job interests are specialized, just so you don't miss the point.

PISCES (on 4th house cusp)
VIRGO (on 10th)
(Sagittarius rising)

Often Cinderella at home, cleaning up after everyone, almost enjoying it! Watch them go after a job though.

Looking for the Anima and Animus

Unlike the archetype of the Shadow, the figures embodying the inner personification of the opposite sex require much more than a simple recognition of their autonomy. They stand further away from consciousness than the Shadow and always make themselves known in a unconscious way, that is, driving us towards actions over which the ego has little control. It is easier to acknowledge our vulnerable areas (personified by the Shadow) than to embrace the totality of the psyche by inclusion of the unconscious, contrasexual view of the male–female role.

Even when one is aware of the presence of this archetype and has recognized its content, there is no integrating it without struggle, for the inner figures that bring man and woman their greatest joy, comfort and ecstasy are the same ones that cause sadness, pain and sorrow. Often they work simultaneously; a man's anima projection onto a female is capable of transporting him into temporary euphoria and at the same time anguish about the thought of ever losing his beloved to another.

The usual house rules to be observed when looking to these figures on the chart are Moon–Venus positions (male) and Sun–Mars positions (female) and we have only begun to learn of these secret powers behind the throne. The anima and animus are little personalities, often with a will all of their own. Referring to the anima/animus tables (Chapter 4), you will observe in the left-hand column the very thing that a person is attracted to in that particular element. On the right-hand side is the repellent face of this expression that occurs when the relationship has leaned too far on one side; then, what was once calming and sympathetic to a male, has become stifling and threatens to suck the life out of him.

The house positions of these planets tell us where this archetypal experience will be found, creeping into the conscious life, dawning on an individual who must make room for this strange and fascinating, yet often frightening creature. 'Typing' the anima may not be as easy as developing an outline for the function of consciousness; obviously there will be charts full of Air, Water, etc., which make it easy to discern where the unconscious other-half is coming from. The Moon is the archetypal mother-love experience and therefore the Sun represents the masculine side of this coin. Venus is the experience of woman-love, and Mars is found in the female psyche as the energy that goads her into the need to discover herself as a sexual being in her own right, making the transition from the daughter of the father to the wife-lover of the partner.

In order to arrive at a conscious relationship, these figures ought not to be allowed completely to dictate the rules of the game. The difficulty here is the compulsive and obsessive element that they bring, especially within the first two or three months of a new relationship. With the progress of time, the spell wears off a little and if one can begin to see the partner in their real light, a relationship can be built on a mutual recognition of each other's true selves.

Projecting the Planets

The general methods of horoscopic interpretation lead the practising astrologer into a complex field of planet–sign–house–aspect correlation so vast and confusing that it is often difficult to know exactly where to start. Does one begin with the most highlighted and obvious areas or not? It may well be that there are are areas on the chart being used that do not show up so visibly, until the chart has been discussed in full with the individual themselves. The planetary principles, having once been digested, are applied to the sign and house in which they fall, and for the astrological student there is a full list of keywords in Appendix I for those practising basic astrology. One can never really 'know' everything there is to know of the planetary effects unless one has experienced the energies through all of the different permutations of signs and houses. Sometimes an intellectual knowledge will have to suffice.

A projection is an act of seeing what one has created from an inner source, so that we are likely to 'see' the effects of that particular planet working through an astrological house. This section is thus dedicated to a Jungian approach of projecting the planetary archetypes through the houses.

Seeing the Sun
The house containing the Sun is where we see our own specialness, creation of self and take pride in the objects associated with it. One will find the 'father archetype' there too, perhaps representing the things we have been encouraged to bring out of us.

Examples: 1st. Pride in one's appearance, oneself. 3rd. Pride in one's education, conversation, book collection. 4th, seeing one's home as a special, important place, and therefore something to be proud of.

Seeing the Moon
Seeing the Moon in a house means seeing the mother archetype at work; here is where we look for a source of comfort or see the need for it. Observe the malleability of this house, the feeling-toned complexes and the archetypal 'mother' inheritances.

Examples: 1st. Seeing the need for acceptance by others, receptivity and natural response. 5th. Seeing the need for creative ego-expression. 6th. Seeing the need for routine, order and cleanliness, feeling better after you've scrubbed the house.

Seeing Mercury
Mercury is a learning and communicating archetype; therefore if you can grasp the idea of 'seeing communication' in a house, in all its varied forms, then you have the basic imprint of Mercury.

Examples: 1st. Seeing oneself as a studious, communicative type. 6th. Seeing the intellectual aspects of work, productivity and self-management. (Thus, these types often read and talk about work a lot, whether or not they actually do any is another matter.)

Seeing Venus

Venus is the easiest to grasp when discussed in this particular light, because one merely sees the refinement, beauty and grace of Venus through each of the houses.

Examples: 1st. Seeing beauty in oneself. 2nd. Beauty in material objects. 3rd. Beauty in words, verbal expressions, etc. 4th. Beauty in one's home. And so on and so forth.

Seeing Mars

Seeing Mars in a house means visions of action, competitiveness and dynamism—even if there is no real battlefield out there after all—one is ready for a challenge.

Examples: 1st. Seeing onself as active, energetic and wilful. 4th. Seeing the domestic scene as a potential battlefield, competition to be boss at home, etc. 7th. Partnerships as an arena filled with verve and excitement, provoking a competitive attitude to relationships.

Seeing Jupiter

To 'see' Jupiter in a house is to use blind faith and use your generous, benevolent spirit—thus visions of good luck and protection—after all we are only getting back what we have already given out.

Examples: 1st. Seeing oneself as a lucky, generous type. 4th. Seeing one of the parents as a happy-go-lucky individual. 10th. Seeing one's career as an expansive, opportunist environment and not just a little fortunate for oneself.

Seeing Saturn

When we observe the effects of Saturn we are often seeing the results of our own fear, projected on to the house he is placed in, often goading us into the need for self-protection and overcompensation. We are also seeing the Shadow, but as if it didn't belong to us.

Examples: 1st. Seeing oneself as cautious, responsible and hard-working (often used as a disguise to cover up one's own fear of expressing oneself freely). 3rd. Seeing communication as a very heavyweight affair, often finding difficulty with light conversation and small talk.

Perhaps we need to put a few points into perspective here; the personal planets can only be felt or seen (in a metaphorical sense) through the houses when there is sufficient awareness of their energies. Since Jupiter and Saturn are collective principles, we are approaching thin ground for actually observing their effects with any clarity. That being so, the three outermost planets can exude only a dim awareness through the individual psyche, unless sensitively placed on angles or strongly aspecting personal planets. When this happens, they require patience if they are to be dealt with in any conscious fashion, for they keep cropping up when you don't want them to.

Consider Pluto placed on the MC of an individual who cannot understand why all of his ex-employers have been dogmatic, power-mad tyrants; not a pleasant situation to have to deal with. But it is the individual unconscious attitude to authority that is doing the work. Part of his inner nature is Plutonian and makes its own demands for personal power, therefore there are his own seeds of tyranny and thirsts for conquest to consider. Perhaps as a child, this individual was exposed to parents who ruled the roost with a rod of iron, cracking the whip to discipline him in teenage years, and he's not going to forget it that easily. This memory is lurking beneath consciousness, dictating much of his attitudes to those in authority and now he inwardly declares that no one is going to wave their power over his head ever again. Hence the projection onto the people under whom he has worked.

Finding the Shadow
There is a basic psychological premise that whenever we act out of fear, trying to protect ourselves, immediately we call forth the notion that we must be in danger. This is so stupidly simple that we are likely to feel less afraid by simply not acting at all, thus suggesting to ourselves that there is no real danger anyway. It may sound a little bloated to some individuals to hear that there is nothing to fear but fear itself, but this is Saturn's superb illusion—he makes you think that the fear is real because you lose perspective on the situation.

Fear does strange things to people and invites a host of playful inner demons to tea, making you think that everything is falling apart in your life. All of those little structures you've built patiently, carefully planning their design meticulously and attentively are suddenly threatened, thus sparking off a life-or-death attitude as you spring into action trying to preserve your precious piece of work, whether it be a job, relationship or the family unit. You must stay in control!

Saturn is really the illusion of reality, and his placement on the chart denotes such austere and sober attitudes to life, born out of the wall built to hide our deepest fears and weaknesses. The trouble is, we build that wall too thick, and any structure that is meant to be permanent needs 'give' in it. Cars and buildings provide a pretty good example. What about those little flaws of ours then?

The Shadow often forms a major organ of the inferior function. Saturn's position by sign and house often points to qualities that are the very antithesis of the superior function, and are therefore the unconscious, weak points in the human psyche. It is common for an individual to dislike intensely others who possess the qualities of his Saturn area in their superior function, because it is difficult to express in himself as a conscious element.

Look to your own Saturn areas (sign, house and aspects) and you will arrive at the place in which you feel thwarted or cut off from the mainstream, and then ask yourself this question: What are the qualities I dislike most in others? Nine times out of ten you will have described the element in which Saturn is placed by sign or house. The person onto which your Shadow projection falls is doing what comes naturally to him, expressing qualities associated with the superior function of which he is conscious. Energies that you find difficult to express constantly annoy you in the other person.

Saturn is often associated with parents on the birth chart when an individual has felt to be held back from progressing in life. I personally do not consider Saturn as having a great deal to do with either of the parents, yet experience has shown that one's mother and father have unfortunately received the ugly projection of Saturn. Since Saturn limits and structures, he is projected onto either parent as a binding, restrictive influence, though obviously, not everyone has narrow-minded, strict parents. The child or youth resisting the energy of Saturn looks to the most obvious source of restriction and by the expulsion of Saturn's contents onto the most likely object, manages to clothe the parents with his own projection. I suspect that children and teenagers developing without strict parental guidance never project Saturn onto either parent if they have had positive experiences of upbringing and thought their developing years to be utterly beneficial and protective.

A great deal can be found in aspects where Saturn contacts either the Sun or Moon, often pointing to difficulties with parents, poor upbringing and in many cases an absence of either the mother or father. Too many times I have seen a Moon–Saturn opposition where either the parents had divorced or one of them had passed away. In most cases the mother was not present at home and the individual had inherited a difficulty with their inner feeling nature, represented by the Moon. They had become stunted in their emotional development and were often cut off from their inner emotions, finding great difficulty in spontaneous feeling expression. Saturn had closed off that particular channel making them extremely vulnerable underneath, but outwardly appearing self-contained and certainly in no need of loving comfort from anyone, while in fact this is the very thing they crave the most.

The Often Unwelcome Gods—Archetypal Patterns of the Outer Planets

Bound up in the fabric of what we like to call fate are the energies of planets that require patience and understanding if they are to help us grow on a psychological level. They are the gods Uranus, Neptune and Pluto, and their positions on the birth chart are subject to the same 'fated' pattern that only penetrates into consciousness during crisis periods or spells of fruitful change. At normal periods, they are more or less under lock and key, but they do turn up in some interesting places, often analogous to the personality of an individual.

Consider the strong Earthy woman, a sensation type fond of security, and the need to possess and be in control. But there is Uranus in her seventh house demanding expression and personal freedom; it is typical for a strong sensation type to resist such a planet as Uranus since he threatens to disrupt the very foundations upon which Earthiness is built. Then fate intervenes and it is once again, the 'other' person.

Consider Neptune in the third house of a typical thinking type whose chart predominates with Gemini and Aquarius—both signs that are fond of rationalizing and logical thinking. Neptune here seems like an omnipresent shadow, only a moment away, ready to flood consciousness and dissolve all of one's tried and trusted positive thinking. This planet is the antithesis of the Air function who is fond of a rational, reasonable scheme of ideas upon which he can base life. Neptune (to him) will only cloud the issues and lead him into a fog. If this planet is not allowed to see the light of day, he will surface in projections and to the individual, it will appear that there are certain people 'out there' who are stupidly vague and unrealistic, over-sentimental and gushing.

This is the sort of thing that happens when there are outer planets on the chart radically out of tune with the usual frequency of consciousness. Yet they must be looked at and integrated. They are gods who are alive and well, living in the psyche's deepest region but often felt to be uncomfortable, awkward and threatening. This is because they represent urges that are often beyond the limits of daily living; they are quite removed from mundane, everyday reality. We are only human and cannot easily make room for such energies that are to do either with sudden change, gradual, unworldly change or drastic, irrevocable change. The planets symbolizing these energies are Uranus, Neptune and Pluto respectively. Only at certain intense periods of your life will these energies be felt, usually through an external situation. Then, the flowering of that planet's energy will be recognized.

These three planets assist in the process of individuation, which is a pattern of growth that calls upon all four functions of consciousness to be integrated, developed and thus allowing a more rounded-out, finely balanced personality. If this happens at all, it usually occurs after the age of 40, when the inferior function begins to work its way into consciousness and thus develop in its own right.

Jung likened the psyche to that of an actual organ of the body, which is made up of subtler organs that, like the body, must maintain equilibrium for the whole structure to function healthily. Four such 'organs' are the psychological types; there is often a sensitive imbalance within this fourfold scheme, the individual relying heavily on at least two of the functions for 'getting by'. With the least accessible function remaining undeveloped up until about middle age, the psyche is often at pains to allow any new life to enter, feeling relatively safe with the ego—but the outer planets will see to it that creative change *does* occur.

To Uranus, life must be dynamic, fresh, exciting and contain lots of changes. His position on the chart denotes the area in which life must be invigorating; as soon as that area of life seems dull, you're off like a shot to create something new in its place. You won't be tied down here by anyone, you need to be able to please yourself what you will do, and when you will do it. From a Jungian point of view, the spirit of man (or woman) must be allowed to roam: each one is a unique entity and if that uniqueness is thwarted or suppressed, the unconscious becomes very angry indeed, seeking revenge through the architects of fate—one of which is the Uranus archetype. When we don't use our Uranus therefore, other people do it to us.

To Neptune, life is not enclosed within structure, everything ceaselessly flows in and flows out of the great oceanic universe where we are all one. This suggests an ideal universe, nirvana, utopia, a blissful heavenly state where everything remains that way. No wonder stiff upper-lip Saturnians or aggressive Martians run like hell when they hear the word Neptune. Wherever he is found on the birth chart is (like Uranus) unconscious and therefore operating out of sight, hidden from the normal view of the ego and slowly eroding its way into one's everyday reality, as opposed to Uranus' blinding flash. Imagine what he does to someone who cannot even begin to perceive of another 'reality' or even an unconscious mind. One of the tricks Neptune employs is deception and subtle evasion.

On the positive side, his area on the chart is one in which you create a perfect ideal, a dream for the future or to have the things of that particular house in an ideal state. Unfortunately many people entertain such illusions under the impression that they are readily attainable; even ones who are not so misguided are often disillusioned in however small a way, because their idealizing left out the hard-nosed realities that come with any situation.

In a Jungian sense, the idealizing about life that comes with Neptune is only the tip of the trident, if you'll pardon the expression. At the deepest recesses of the psyche, there lurks somewhere an urge to reconnect with the source from whence we come—water. Neptunian vibes are concerned with the urge to re-enter this blissful state and thus become one once again with the waters of life. To us on a material level, it is translated as a kind of idealizing about a perfect world, usually a dream landscape that cannot exist here and now in the gloomy, concrete jungle of normality.

To Pluto, life is death and death is life, killing the living and living to kill; but it is unfair to suggest that Pluto thrives on the pain of others. Certainly he causes pain, suffering and burning melancholia but he is beyond any sinister motive. Death is never a nice word, even insurance salesmen will not be so unkind as to utter the frightful five-letter word, so they use the clichéd, sugar-coated premise that 'if anything should happen . . .' Death is a part of nature, therefore inevitable. I once remember reading a cartoon joke, the type that appears in the tabloids each day and in it, two insurance men had just exited the house of their visibly angry housewife customer. The elderly one turned to his puzzled and rather inexperienced colleague and remarked '. . . And you're supposed to say, "if anything should happen", not "and when the old trout snuffs it"!'

With Pluto on the chart, there is a succession of deaths occurring in that house throughout life. In mundane terms, it means an area of life that is stop-start—in effect, an area through which you perceive the changing face of the regenerative process. An area that is 'killed off' in order for something more vital and important to flourish. Will it be a job? (tenth house); a relationship (seventh house); your social circles? (eleventh house); or your personal finances? (second house).

Let's look at this syndrome of something being 'killed off' because that's what Pluto is really all about and let's not panic at the thought of the word 'kill'. Life can only repeat itself through growth and when something has finished growing, it must die—herein lies the essence of the Plutonian effect on the houses.

How can for instance Pluto kill off and renew in either our second, sixth or ninth houses? The former two are completely materialistic and mundane, the latter is a house of the higher mind—Pluto wants to go in the opposite direction. An individual with Pluto in the second, over a course of one lifetime will reassess his values about material objects; I would imagine that various possessions are likely to be stripped away from him at various times or he incurs the loss of a major amount of his own money. Within the bowels of his own unconscious is his own urge to eliminate attachment to material objects, not eliminate the objects themselves. His inner Pluto archetype desires to be free of the ego's attachment to materialistic things. Unconsciously he does not value them and so the unconscious programmes an external event in order to get rid of some of them. If at the conscious level, he is a particularly possessive or worse still, hedonistic type—he is in for a nervous breakdown.

Pluto in the sixth 'kills off' another form of material attachment, your valuing of the work that you perform and any ego-gratification it may bring. Pluto in the sixth individuals may have trouble coping with wilful and difficult employees or become intensely dissatisfied with the way their routine is put together. Things bound up in usual, everyday reality seem to go drastically wrong, maintaining a level of normality may be difficult or there are severe ailments surfacing within the physical body. To the extent that we are tied to duty and necessity, we will feel stamped upon when the system develops a malfunction. This is particularly true with one's health. Pluto sixth-housers probably refuse to be ill—even when they're nearly dropping. What the unconscious is doing is trying to relieve the ego of the burden of too much identification with structure, encompassing as it does everyday routine, order, duty, maintenance and service to others. Thus killing off the limiting attachment to one's routine work environment.

With Pluto in the ninth house there is a vast difference in attitude, but he is still essentially acting as jury, executioner and resurrectioner.

In the house of one's philosophical ideas, he can do nothing save to bring them down to his own unconscious level before he can start to penetrate. You cannot penetrate something that is essentially up in the air and wants to fly away. One attaches Pluto to a particular philosophy and then runs the risk of seeing a religious or political view slashed to pieces by an untruth, spoken through the lips of another, be it satirist, moralist or atheist. Therefore, one's obsessive views about ninth house matters are challenged when they are stuck rigidly and firmly in one's consciousness. They are threatened by someone else's opposing views or philosophies, often making the Pluto ninth-houser even more inclined to cling to his philosophy or religion and turn more dogmatic in the process. 'Aha, it is they who are trying to rob me of my precious religious views by insulting our leader' says ninth house Pluto. Remember with Pluto, it's kill-off and renew time.

A Word (or Two) about Aspects

God invented aspects to make astrology even more complicated, so let's try to break things down a little. The Sun in Taurus in the seventh house quincunx to the Moon in Sagittarius in the second house is too much to go at all at once. Begin with the combined nature of the two planets involved. What do the Sun and Moon mean when they come together in a chart? Regardless of aspect, the cookbooks will explain this, but I would recommend a book called *Horoscope Symbols* by American Robert Hand (Para Research) for further reading, which contains a list of planetary pairs. It is an excellent example of modern astrology expressed through the symbols of antiquity.

Having digested the third party, that is, the result of the combination of the two planets, it is relatively easy to apply the nature of the aspect between the two bodies. For soft aspects, there will be an easy fusion, communication and expression. With hard aspects there will be exaggeration, resistance and conflict aroused between the two principles. Having done that, note the signs and houses between which the aspect occurs, sign for expression and house for where that aspect is 'seen' to occur and make its presence felt.

Four Types of Chart

The four natal charts shown on pages 114-15 are examples of my own research into the phenomena of Carl Jung's typology. All four waver slightly during the expression of the main function, alternating with the auxiliary function that falls into place when it is called upon.

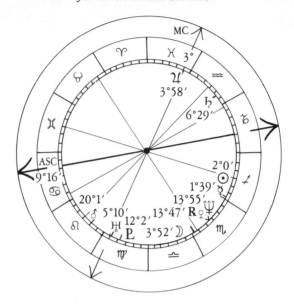

Chart A: An Intuitive Type

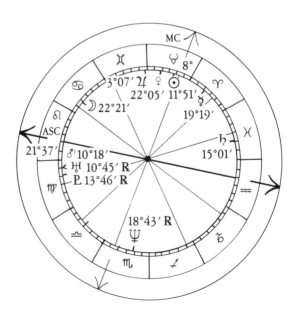

Chart B: A Sensation Type

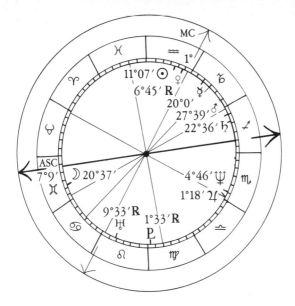

Chart C: A Thinking Type

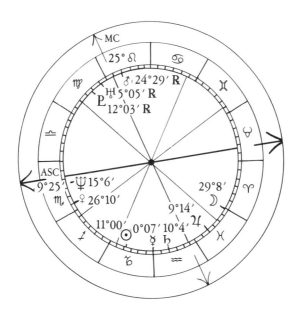

Chart D: A Feeling Type

I was able to determine the anima/animus and Shadow archetypes from all four, having observed these individuals either in consultation or at close quarters for a lengthy period. Each chart is of a different model, functioning according to its superior element. Chart A is a male chart of the intuitive type expressing as it does, the typical Fiery temperament—expectancy, optimism and a characteristic devil-may-care attitude to life. This is one instance where I could not use the ascendant as a starting point in order to determine the main function, but it is sprinkled with enough clues to lead one to assume that intuition is present.

NB: I have observed the general rule that if a planet falls within 5° to 6° of the following house cusp, then it appears to weaken in the preceding house. Some of these charts have certainly stood up to that rule in my observations of these individuals and the planet concerned affects the next house most strongly.

Note the Sun, Mercury and Mars in the Fire signs Sagittarius and Leo, strong indications as to the native's own animus figure—that is his own expression of the masculine principle. Here it is somewhat idealistic, forward-looking and freedom-loving. There are three planets in Scorpio, all pertaining to the inner soul figure, both the Moon and the Venus–Neptune conjunction are in the fifth house, giving those planets a dramatic but sensitive quality—already we have the effect of Fire and Water coming together in the same person. The Sun–Mercury conjunction in Fire signs in a Fiery house is even more indicative of an intuitive; also note Jupiter (predominantly a Fire planet) on the MC which makes the Jupiter principle one of this person's major aims in life—he is cultivating more and more Jupiterian qualities.

This person has a keen wit, a developed sense of showmanship and the need to express himself in a creative, sometimes attention-seeking manner, a strong fifth house influence if ever there was one. The anima planets fall in this region too; the Venus/Neptune conjunction in Watery Scorpio creates an idealized image of languid erotic beauty—the perfect image stemming from Neptune, and a 'Scorpionic' anima would definitely be very sexy and mysterious.

The Moon in Scorpio only adds more depth and tone to the inner image. His so-called unconscious areas fall in the Saturn regions and the usual rule-of-thumb for deriving one of them—the sign on the cusp of the seventh house.

One must also not forget the houses into which the transpersonal planets fall—in this case, the fourth and fifth houses (the fifth seems to be an exception in this case, as there is a preponderance of personal planets).

With Saturn in the eighth, there is an eighth house Shadow, shunning any deep emotional commitments for fear of bondage of one's soul; this person feels the need to preserve his ego identity (fifth house) and does not easily make such binding emotional commitments (eighth house). Another fact that may be pointed out is that these two houses are in square to each other, thus the principles they represent will resist one another. This is precisely what happens here with an eighth house Saturn and a fifth house Sun.

There is a lack of both Earth and Air, but since the emphasis veers slightly away in favour of Fire, the sensation function is weakest. In fact this person is typical of the faults associated with so much Fire: rash, impulsive behaviour, accident-proneness and a general disregard for the material world in favour of the ideal. There is a great deal of physical energy and boisterousness, having been channelled into creative pastimes, sport and writing, all pointing once again to a fifth house, intuitive type.

The second chart, B, is that of a female sensation type—the polar opposite you might say of chart A. On first glance the Leo ascendant may betray this but on closer inspection one can see that it is the only Fiery element that appears, apart from cold Mercury. The individual in question displays all of the usual Leo rising qualities which you might expect: a bright, cheerful and sunny demeanour, affection displayed generously, pride and a slight trace of pomposity. Nothing too damaging, of course. But, the usual inventiveness and zeal of the Fire signs is nowhere else to be found, the chart being heavily weighed in favour of staid, preserving Taurus (Sun, Venus, MC). Sun in the tenth and Moon in Cancer almost deliberately ties her to the bondage of parents, so that the parents axis has considerable influence over her every move in the outside world. Both of her parents are earth signs so that the subject identifies with practical, commonsense reality (as an inheritance from the mother and father archeytpes) to the exclusion of the inner meanings and vision about everyday life. Some would undoubtedly find this person a little 'ordinary' since there is not much lived out through her that goes beyond a job, a table in a restaurant and the living room settee.

She looks for excitement in a male partner and assigns to him the responsibility for bringing liveliness and spontaneity into her life. One main point is that she is heavily tied to the parental cord; it is they who 'know best', they who crack the whip at home whilst she does precisely as she is told (Scorpio on the fourth cusp containing Neptune).

There is a further emphasis on earth with the Mars–Uranus–Pluto conjunction in Virgo in the latter stages of the first house. This shows some of her extreme determination to 'make it' in the real world and it must be said that she is an extremely capable and hardworking type. The conjunction is accentuated by the opposition from Saturn, creating a stop-start syndrome that results in inner frustrations and unexpressed rage that is projected onto the parents. Here, there is another eighth house Shadow, as in chart A, that results in a fear of succumbing to emotional chaos and being swept away with the tide while she retains a foothold with the planets in Virgo.

The Moon at the cusp of the twelfth is another 'shadowy' area that manifests as difficulties with the mother, expelling deep, irrational undercurrents that often cause chaos at home. The mother is prone to violent displays of temper that wreak havoc on the home front, causing scenes of the most unpleasant kind. To be exposed to this type of occurrence is typical for the individual with a poorly, un-lived out twelfth house Moon and it is worth wondering exactly who is projecting onto whom. So we can safely assume that the Shadow is Watery; there is very little Fire and very little Air.

The Aquarius on the seventh house cusp is unconscious, pertaining to the animus, and with the Sun and Mars in Earth signs one might assume a type of father-teacher figure. As a matter of fact, it works in practice too; this person is attracted to strongly intellectual men (or at least, men whom she believes to be intellectual) who can provide fun and excitement, a witty repartee but most importantly, *security*! The animus image is thus a cross between Earth and Air—the positive, security-orientated builder, attempting to use his manipulative skills to reach the top of the ladder. Mother would be *so* proud.

Chart C is a thinking type, perhaps one of the more obvious charts to spur an immediate impression of the main function. This is a female individual, possessed of the usual butterfly-like Geminian qualities but encased in a hard-nosed, reality-orientated attitude. Observe the Mars–Saturn conjunction that opposes a first house Moon; the feelings here do not give way so easily and it is characteristic of this individual to rationalize about emotion. Beneath this attitude is the Saturnian self-defence of what it considers to be a vulnerable area, and she makes an excellent job of compensating for a dormant feeling faculty with the Sun, Moon, Venus and the ascendant in Air.

Much valuing done by the persona is incapable of perceiving the hidden undercurrents and feeling implications in a personal situation, disregarding the emotional content in others and lumping everyone together under a great collective tag. It is this impersonal approach to people that allows her to scrutinize them in a flat, scientific manner, very much typical of strong Aquarius.

The Moon/Mars–Saturn opposition has left her feeling awkward about displaying emotion and she is apt to be very apprehensive about releasing these inner feeling states; this inner dynamic determines much of her approach to the animus figure which contains Airy and Fiery energies. The Shadow archetype resides in the seventh house and together with the animus, is representative of her attractions to those of the opposite sex. Unconsciously, the animus draws her into relationship with the gifted intellectual, the thinker and scholar who cares about society and who can give opinions that are honest and just.

Her choice of partners have confirmed this, and as soon as she felt herself becoming 'involved' with them on a feeling level, the Shadow would awaken to life and demand expression. She would rely on her thinking function and project Saturn onto the relationship, complaining that it was too 'heavy' and 'demanding'. The obvious hook on which to hang her shadow picture was any number of males who could first attract her through Airy qualities like her Sun–Venus conjunction in Aquarius. She found herself drawn to men with strong humanitarian values, powerful speakers and males who could make interesting intelligent conversation.

The opposition was triggered off in these partnerships and the same dark beast reared its ugly head. Only later was she to discover that most of these men were prone to aggressive, emotional storms and while they did not actually physically abuse her, their destructive words were sufficient to cause irreparable damage to the relationship.

Although outwardly, these individuals appeared to possess a gift for intellectual prowess and a marked degree of individuality, most of what she found attractive about them was in fact her own creation. The qualities she imbued them with were born out of the power of her own stubborn projection. Many of her previous partners were in essence, feeling types of the sensitive kind and ranged in mood, swinging from the very low to the very high. They would display a boisterousness and ebullience that would soon dissolve into introspection and seriousness—two aspects of the Moon opposition; first to Mars (high energy) and then to Saturn (limited energy). She discovered qualities that she very much disliked in them; a typical Shadow projection, yet for some reason was strangely drawn to such people. It does not surprise me to find that in her relationships, she elicited an aspect of raw feeling and unwanted emotion with such an emphasis of thinking factors present on the birth chart.

Outwardly, she expresses an easy grace and charm where communication is concerned, combined with an ambitious drive to succeed; needless to say, her talents lie in the area of public related matters. On the last occasion that I performed a reading for her, she was starting work for a large governmental body as an administrative assistant in the Equal Opportunities Commission. This enhances my theory that the Sun is often a reliable indicator of career choice. How very apt for this person to opt for a vocation associated with equal rights with a chance to work her way up the management ladder (Sun in Aquarius, tenth house).

Finally we arrive at chart D, very much the other face of the previous chart and at first glance pretty much what you'd expect, a feeling type. This male chart has Watery Neptune on a Scorpio ascendant, Venus in the first house and a Piscean Moon, all suggesting the need to relate to life intensely emotionally. This person is fond of the emotional drama so typical of Scorpio, exuding a Pluto/Neptune mask for the world to see; the Capricorn Sun provides fertile soil on which to build. The superior element is also easily recognized by a lack of true Air; I say true because although Mercury is placed well in Aquarius, it must bear the lead-like weight of Saturn, pertaining to the Shadow figure. With a shadowy third house, communication is often something of a bind, a restriction and this person lacks the lightness and articulacy usually associated with an Airy temperament, his Shadow falling on those who possess a fuller flow of this element.

The anima figure is the Watery ideal, similar to that of chart A, but here there is an emphasis on the Neptune principle. You could say that this is indeed a romantic inner figure, the Moon in the fifth suggesting the need for love affairs and courtship, but it embraces the whole spectrum of romanticism such as creative imagination, a fondness for art, drama and especially music. This person is fond of writing poetry in order to amplify and express the needs of the fifth house. Venus in Scorpio cements the emotions with passion and a love-hate nature, often denying that there is any difference between the two emotions. Unlike chart A, the finely tuned sensitivities are not so well-hidden; affection is demonstrated much more intently and deliberately.

The Moon as the mother archetype stands for what the individual has gained in reaction to the feminine, but there is also Fiery Mars placed firmly on the MC within one degree. This suggests that this person inherits Fiery instincts from the mother too, and indeed the mother is a pretty volatile creature, senstive, loving, but prone to the odd outburst or two. The Uranus/Pluto conjunction occurs in the neighbouring area of the tenth house, making it difficult to accept discipline and take orders. He must be his own boss if he is to be happy at work, doing it *his* way.

Lastly a word about the seventh house, upon which falls Taurus. The seventh is the area experienced through others in relationships, so that it must form another layer of clothing on the anima, needing stability and security in relationships. But for this person it is rarely translated into material terms, note the Neptune opposite the descendant—it is emotional stability which this person seeks, and as we all know, it begins at home with the fourth house.

Unfortunately there is not room to present a fuller description of these four charts. One could fill the pages of a whole book discussing one chart alone, but I hope I have managed to present a building block on to which one can start to erect a Jungian chart. There are so many factors to take into consideration that I am sometimes at a loss as to where to begin. Each chart is as complex as the individual whom it reflects and contains all of the signs, all of the elements, strengths and weaknesses, cosmically scattered around what we like to call the natal chart.

People change like the wind, and it is observable with the sweeping faces of nature as the background scenery of planets changes every hour, constantly in a state of flux. Those who refuse to go with the flow will experience tension and pressure; wherever there is resistance there is friction. If you work with your birth chart you will be able to observe the changes going on in yourself, out there in the night sky, as the planets symbolically replay your own inner transformation. These developments are recorded between the pages of an ephemeris, using glyphs to denote which planet is which and through which sign they happen to be passing at the moment. (See section on transits, 'The Creative Power of the Unconscious', Chapter 8.)

8.
HOW?

We now enter into a very profound area indeed and raise the issue of the 'how', and to a lesser extent, the 'why' of astrology. Through the ages we have been offered various explanations, ranging from the intervention of divine forces to actual celestial mechanics. There is no need to take a causal approach if you do not so wish. I personally believe that the Sun and Moon are the only bodies likely to affect a human being on earth in physical terms. There can be no reductional explanation for the way in which the planets correlate with our behaviour on earth. The planets are not really out there at all (in a metaphorical sense) but symbolize forces activated within us that behave in the same way.

Maybe you are acquainted with Jung's axiom that whatever happens to a person is characteristic of him; this is such an acute observation that it convolutes the message of astrology into one little sentence. But it does not explain exactly how this should come about. Needless to say, those with a scientific mind will rack their brains demanding a logical answer. The outbreak of intellectualism is pandemic these days and we are, ostensibly, heavily tied to religious dogma and the antiseptic rationalizing of scientists who have yet to learn that nature does not give up her secrets lightly.

On a more realistic level there is no-one going to make a better job of living your life for you than yourself. It is we who are responsible for attracting the things that happen to us and for many this may be a bitter pill to swallow. Our lives are created by our very own minds and there are thousands of self-help and inspirational manuals that propose the benefits of positive thinking, visualization, self-hypnotism and meditation. It is hard not to be inspired in some way to test the power of the subconscious or make ginger attempts at autosuggestion, enthralled after having read one of these books. They sell by the cartload, positively beaming with the message that there is magic in your mind.

All this is not much use though to the woman plagued with marital problems on the brink of a nervous breakdown. Perhaps she'd be better off coming back to the book when she's finished with the tablets. What she really wants to know is how she got into such an uncontrollable mess in the first place. Telling her that it was the work of the unconscious would sound a little unsympathetic to say the least; pathetic seems more appropriate. Nevertheless, this is the sad, unvarnished truth.

For many of us there is a distinct difference between the things that happen to us and the things we do of our own volition, some have described it as fate versus free will. Take fate for example, why do fortunate circumstances fall so easily into our lap that we are convinced that it's a gift from above? Did its happening not have a counterpart somewhere within us, below that surface level which we use to think with?

Life around us is a reflection of our inner natures, that is represented in symbols on the horoscope wheel. Every little thought and impression registers in that mind of ours. We have all experienced the mind's capability of recalling events that happened so long ago that we thought we had completely forgotten about them. Every little act we perform, regardless of what the conscious mind acknowledges at the time, is impressed onto the unconscious and it is here that the real underlying motive for our actions is recorded and acted upon by the creative power down below. We behave in certain ways out of a belief that it is the best thing for us. Even the act of walking is as much an act of faith as it is muscular control. The little things we have faith in; the big things are another matter. What we are not so keen to have faith in, is the intangible, unknowable future.

The Creative Power of the Unconscious

Astrology is a living thing and when we ask, 'How does it work?' we are dealing with the shifting patterns of energy on the birth chart occurring unconsciously as the life of an individual unfolds. Astrology is a tool, implemented to denote the cycle of change at work within us. Transits, which are merely the planets in the sky at this moment passing over your birth chart, are the easiest and most popular tool to work with. If your ascendant is at 15° of Scorpio on the birth chart and Saturn in the sky reaches 15° Scorpio, then the transiting Saturn is conjunct your ascendant until it moves away from the degree. Over a period of about thirty years it will have passed through all of your chart, making every conceivable kind of aspect to your natal planets.

But what's happening out there is only a symbolic representation for what's happening at an unconscious level. The planets denote energies that are enacted simultaneously within us. As a planet aspects one of your natal planets by transit, the two natures combine and so is your psyche affected in those terms. Let's say that Saturn actually does hit your ascendant by conjunction, why the hell do you suddenly fall ill, become depressed or shut yourself away in the bedroom for two weeks? Saturn symbolizes structure, form, concentration and crystallization in any fashion.

He represents the need to structure one's life in the most reliable form available and the ascendant is your outer personality, physical mannerisms and actual body type. This is where we spontaneously put energies out into the world but unconsciously, Saturn wants to build walls and contain those energies during this transit. No wonder that they surface as ailments in the physical body, general fatigue or the desire to be alone. The 'wall' that Saturn builds around the first house in order that one may begin to define one's personality may surface as overt defensive behaviour at this time because you are shutting others out of your world, not always voluntarily. The outer is reflected by the inner and becomes projected on to a real-life situation.

People become weary and depressed with Saturn transits, the unconscious mechanism is to preserve the old psychic structure but also to concentrate energy onto what is really necessary to you. Any situation having outlived its usefulness therefore, will die. This does not mean to say that the particular life situation will necessarily be 'taken away' from you, but that you will notice yourself that the experience has become exhausted and should take steps either to revitalize it or discard it. The usual feeling at the time though, is to want to hang on to an old situation.

Saturn can provoke anxiety and fear of the future. The inner effect is like a 'psychic stunting', so it is no wonder that you feel like you're wearing lead boots with this transit. Your inner state is 'heavy' and the circumstances around you carry a similar weight, everything moving at about half-speed. You are likely to translate this temporary psychological state into everyday terms with 'the car won't work', 'I feel so tired and exhausted', 'what is it that's holding me back?', 'I'd rather just stay in tonight' or 'I've only been here an hour and I'm already shattered'. The world around you is mirroring your inner psychological phase, as the energies find their way into your life situation by projection.

'It's A Small World'—Synchronicity

'Changes occurring within are projected onto the outer landscape', is my personal axiom for 'how' astrology works in terms of events and so-called fated occurrences. Such power of the unconscious is hard to reckon with, yet, does the unconscious actually 'cause' events during our lives? Sure enough, the symbols in astrology mirror the energy that is associated with the effect.

Take for instance the moment when by transit, Jupiter conjuncts or trines your midheaven. Seemingly from out of the blue you are inundated with offers of employment, a chance to travel or the very real opportunity to get ahead in life. Jupiter symbolizes the expansive principle brought about by a state of faith and an attitude of optimism, tolerance and expectancy. Reaching out in this way towards others who may be able to help you progress in life can only mean that at some time you will reap the benefits of such action. The fundamental law of the distribution of energies in the universe works in your favour at this time. Yet it seems so unbelievably lucky, sickening if it is not happening to you. Surely, one must have had to put out various energies now and then before the goodies can fall into one's lap. If this is the case, then there is a great deal going on 'down there' of which we are continually unaware.

If the planets do not 'cause' anything and the unconscious energies do not either, there ought to be something of value in the mirror effect of symbolism. Within this invisible framework is something we call attraction, but do we attract the situation or does the situation attract us? How many times have you read someone's name in a newspaper, only to see them appear on TV that night? How many times have you been talking with a friend about someone known to both of you only to see them suddenly appear? The term for this phenomenon is synchronicity. There must be millions of little coincidences like this happening every day; it is the major coincidences that concern us here.

A meaningful coincidence is one that has great value for the individual concerned; from out of the blue, fate shows its face and we suddenly find ourselves on a different road. We are able to look back upon our past and declare that we were somehow meant to be living in this way. Even those with a troubled mind can at least acknowledge that they are not forever doomed to an unhappy life. Some of us are able to see, in retrospect, that if a certain chance occurrence had not happened, we would not be living life in quite the same way today.

I wonder if I would have taken up astrology, had I not encountered an old schoolfriend of mine, even though I had already acquainted myself with the subject. The seed of encouragement had already been planted but I doubt whether I would have been motivated enough into deep study without the 'chance encounter'. It's as if my meeting him sparked off some inner ambition that had previously lain dormant. My studies began with the simplest of informative remarks: 'Hey, I've seen a shop in the town that sells astrology books.' Up until then, I had little real interest in the subject and certainly no desire to become seriously involved with astrology. What I have often asked myself is, would I have been performing endless birth charts today, if I had not re-encountered that particular friend of mine? Would it have happened another way? And if so, would it have been sooner or later? I raise this question because I have a feeling somewhere inside of me, that I was destined for the subject of astrology anyway, as if it was *meant* to happen.

Events such as chance meetings that can radically alter one's present circumstances, appear to be the work of the gods and are not necessarily indicated on the birth chart at the time (the stranger on a train who is going to publish your song, although you do not know it yet; or the shady character opposite you, that one day you will marry). The next section discusses the invisible being who cannot be seen in this world, is not revealed on the birth chart, yet is someone we hazily perceive as existing, waiting in the wings and nudging us ever so gently back onto the inevitable 'path' when we have strayed.

Never Mind the Fortune-Telling, What about the Self?

If we could predict every event with supreme accuracy that is going to occur in our lives, we would probably go crazy. Everything is bound up in the essence of time, how can we be certain of our future (either through astrological forecasts, tarot divination or scanning the inside of your best china after a session with the Earl Grey), when it is clearly something that has not happened yet? One theory is that all of time happens simultaneously, like someone has speeded up the film projector to an infinite rate and we are all zooming around like busy little ants at breakneck pace. It then goes on to suggest that our everyday consciousness slows all of this activity down in order to differentiate between past and present, thereby gaining a perspective on time. This theory proposes that your future has already happened and soon enough you will arrive at a destined situation whether you like it or not. If our limited consciousness therefore, could be expanded infinitely we would be able to see ourselves living out our own future that has already taken place.

It is as if we view the world through a window whose curtains are drawn except for a small parting where they ought to meet. This symbolizes the limitations of the conscious mind which can only perceive time in a straight line, i.e. past-present-future, but if for an instant those curtains are suddenly drawn back and returned to their original position, we can see the whole landscape outside. A sudden shock is enough to bring about this expanded consciousness when the odour of death is close at hand; in these cases we hear someone saying 'I've just seen my whole life flash before me'. Have our futures really already happened? If so, then the visions of clairvoyants have tuned in to that timeless plane where everything is occurring simultaneously, somewhere in the unconscious regions.

Much of the American self-help literature on mind-power states that the unconscious contains knowledge of your future and the conditions to which it relates, as if it somehow knows what is 'best' for you. In occult text we are told that we are born to certain numbers that denote the particular life path that we have chosen. To the sceptical mind it must sound as if the human being is impotent in the face of such awesome control.

Yet there is some indescribable 'thing' within us that in a way guides our actions and makes its presence known with the passing of time, having purpose and meaning for the individual who cares enough to look for it. This is Jung's concept of the Self and I cannot resist equating it with what the man off the street calls 'God', the Chinese sage calls 'the Tao', or way of all nature, and with what one enlightened soul once called the 'beautiful creator'. The Self, it appears, will sometimes unfold contrary to the ego's wishes and then, there is no choice but to go along with what is happening; who knows where it will lead to? It often feels as if we are being shifted around like small boats on a large ocean, but often there is a design, a plan, an actual purpose to all of our ups and downs as we toil on the sea of life.

One typical reflection is that 'there is something to all of this' and life is meaningful after all. Maybe whatever it is that happens in your life is meant to happen, because the Self has decided that it's part of your own blueprint or you needed it to happen in order to learn from the experience, not out of karma, but because what you've just learned will soon prove to be indispensable (an extremely common occurrence as far as fate goes). Is there some wise being inside of us then, who somehow 'knows' what's best for us even if we don't? It often seems that way when undergoing the trial and error syndrome of accomplishment, acquiring knowledge and creative endeavours.

The famous names of history who have given the world her inventions will have called upon the wisdom of the inner self at some time or other, especially when inspiration was lacking. Some of them even gave up half-way, positively drained of creativity, only to find the solution to their problem in a dream, or when they had simply 'let go' and ceased trying to think. Who gave them their answer? And were they 'meant' to find it? I leave it to you.

I have only one final question to ask: Why are we doing all of this?

APPENDIX I
BASIC ASTROLOGY

Signs of the Zodiac with Keywords

1st ARIES
Energetically, Assertively, Independently

2nd TAURUS
Materially, Practically, Possessively

3rd GEMINI
Communicatively, Adaptably, Intellectually

4th CANCER
Emotionally, Protectively, Maternally

5th LEO
Creatively, Dramatically, Nobly

6th VIRGO
Discriminatively, Realistically, Versatilely

7th LIBRA
Fairly, Relatively, Harmoniously

8th SCORPIO
Intensely, Secretively, Excessively

9th SAGITTARIUS
Freely, Optimistically, Generously

10th CAPRICORN
Ambitiously, Conventionally, Cautiously

11th AQUARIUS
Collectively, Coolly, Detachedly

12th   PISCES
Sensitively, Compassionately, Unworldly

Keywords for Planets

☉ SUN   Male principle, Creative power, Energy, Where you are 'going in life', Talents, Leadership

☽ MOON   Female principle, Feelings, Your emotional anchor, Instincts, Food preferences, Domestic affairs

☿ MERCURY   Talking, Thinking, Writing, Travel, Education, The conscious mind

♀ VENUS   Relationships, Pleasures, What turns you on, Romantic love, Aesthetic tastes

♂ MARS   Ego drive, Energy, Independence, Bravery, Activity, Sex drive, Competition, Aggression

♃ JUPITER   Providence, How you have faith, Generosity, Protection, Philosophy, Long-range travel, Opportunity

♄ SATURN   What you are afraid of, Stability, The material world, Delays, Trial and error, Loneliness, Rigidity, Control

♅ URANUS   Sudden change, Freedom, Unconventionality, Truth, Brotherhood, Humanitarianism, Causes, Politics

♆ NEPTUNE   Idealism, Imagination, Spiritual realms, Escapism, Glamour, Sensation, Universal love, Self-sacrifice

♇ PLUTO   Regeneration, Transformation, Death, Unconscious powers, The underworld, Compulsions, Intense feeling

The Horoscope Houses

FIRST HOUSE. Physical appearance, The ego, Health and Vitality, Outward mannerisms, The persona, Childhood (together with the fourth house).

SECOND HOUSE. Money, Possessions, Security, Values in the material world, Food (as a source of pleasure), Sense of self-worth, Possessive qualities.

THIRD HOUSE. Education, The conscious mind, Thinking, Communication, One's everyday normal routine (with regard to communicating), Short journeys, Reading, Writing, Telephones, Neighbours, Brothers, Sisters.

FOURTH HOUSE. Home life, The father (as a rule), One's upbringing, Emotional security, The need to 'belong somewhere', Land, Real estate, One's personal world.

FIFTH HOUSE. Creativity, Children, The love you have to give, How you have fun, Gambling, Speculation, Entertainment, Love affairs, Childlike qualities.

SIXTH HOUSE. Work, One's everyday normal routine (with regard to organization, etc.), Orderliness and duty, Health, Food (as a source of nutrition), Attitude to those in a lesser rank.

SEVENTH HOUSE. One-to-one relationships, Marriage, Partnerships, Open enemies, Public relations, Other people (regarding one's projections).

EIGHTH HOUSE. Shared feelings, Deep emotional encounters with others, Sex (in its emotional aspect as opposed to the pursuit of pleasure, which is the domain of the 5th house), Psychology, Shared resources, Transformation, Crisis, Death.

NINTH HOUSE. Aspiration, Search for meaning, Philosophies, Religion, Foreign travel, Dreams, The law, Politics, Spiritual and other ideals.

TENTH HOUSE. Career life, The mother (as a rule), One's attitude to authority, Ambitions, Social prestige, Worldly values.

ELEVENTH HOUSE. The collective principle, Groups of friends, Clubs, Societies, Humanitarian values.

TWELFTH HOUSE. Unworldly values, Ego sacrifice, Seclusion, Places of confinement, Escapism, The unconscious.

The Aspects

Aspect	Angle	Glyph	Orb	Definition
CONJUNCTION	0°	☌	0-9°	Depends on planets involved, but powerful
SEMI-SEXTILE	30°	⋎	1-2°	Slightly difficult
SEMI-SQUARE	45°	∟	1-2°	Slightly difficult
SEXTILE	60°	★	4-5°	Potentially favourable
SQUARE	90°	☐	9-10°	Obstacles to overcome
TRINE	120°	△	9-10°	Harmonious, favourable
QUINCUNX	150°	⚻	2-3°	Strain
OPPOSITION	180°	☍	9-10°	Conflict, awareness

APPENDIX II
GLOSSARY OF ASTROLOGICAL TERMS

ASCENDANT. The sign rising on the eastern horizon as seen from the place of birth at the moment of birth.

ASPECT. The angular distance measured between two bodies as seen on the ecliptic.

CELESTIAL SPHERE. An imaginary sphere, around which is the belt of the ecliptic and the celestial equator. This sphere contains the movements of all the planets and other bodies.

DECLINATION. The distance in degrees, north or south of the equator.

DESCENDANT. The point directly opposite to the ascendant.

ECLIPTIC. The sun's apparent path, which is actually the plane of the earth's orbit around the Sun.

GMT. Greenwich Mean Time, used as a reference point when calculating, having a longitude of 0.00.

IC/MC. The MC denotes the place on the ecliptic where the sun is found at midday as the earth rotates on its axis. It is the point of culmination in the heavens that begins at the ascendant at sunrise and reaches its peak when the sun is at its highest point in the heavens in the 24 hours earth/sun relationship. The IC is where the sun is found at midnight.

MERIDIAN. There are great lines dividing the globe, running vertically from north to south through the poles that divide the earth into longitudes, then measured from east to west to determine the longitude of the place of birth. The meridian of place of birth then is the point of longitude overhead.

NADIR.   (See Zenith)

ORB.   Used as a guide for how many degrees to allow either side of an exact aspect.

SIDEREAL TIME.   Since actual clock-time varies in minutes on a twenty-four-hour basis, one of the fixed stars is used to refer to instead of the earth's revolution around the sun. The star will appear to be fixed only because it is much further away than the sun. A more or less constant relationship is maintained by measuring the time it takes for the earth to complete one revolution around one of the fixed stars, hence sidereal or star time. Its difference from clock time is recorded in the ephemeris each day, either at noon or midnight.

TRANSIT.   The movements of the planets in the sky at the present time as they appear on the birth chart of an individual. If I have the sun at 15° of Scorpio on my natal chart and Saturn is presently moving through Scorpio in the heavens, when it reaches 15° it will be transiting my natal sun by conjunction.

ZENITH.   The point on the celestial sphere immediately above the birthplace of an individual. Strictly speaking, it is the culmination point on the celestial sphere. The nadir is its opposite, the lowest point in the heavens.

ZODIAC.   A belt of sky encircling the celestial sphere/equator and extending to approximately 9° either side of the ecliptic.

APPENDIX III
GLOSSARY OF JUNGIAN TERMINOLOGY

ANIMA. The female personification of the unconscious often met in dreams, fantasies and is the muse of many great poets, authors, painters and songwriters. She belongs to the realm of the collective unconscious, is difficult to deal with in everyday life because of her autonomy and is projected onto an actual woman during lifetime. The animus is the reverse role in the female unconscious, a more impersonal figure however, projected onto a living male. Their effects are intense during an 'in-love' spell, producing an inexhaustible range of emotions.

ARCHETYPE. An empty structure after which life-forms are patterned when the archetype becomes filled with content. An image or vessel through which life can be portrayed. Robin Hood is one example of an archetypal hero. (See Planetary Archetypes, Ch. 4.)

CONSCIOUSNESS. That which is made aware by the ego on entering the mind becomes conscious and accepted. That which cannot be consciously acknowledged becomes subliminal and unrecognized. To be aware of any given factor, subjective or objective as it arises, is to become conscious of it; the rest remains unconscious, although some of the content may be made conscious.

EGO. The regulating centre of the conscious mind that directs awareness to a given factor, either subjective or objective that is limited in the sense that it can only be aware of one set of circumstances at one time. It is a differentiating function for the purposes of conscious adaptation and control.

EXTROVERSION. The tendency to direct one's energy to the external, objective environment thus continually relying on outside factors for stimulus. There is usually an alternation between extroverted and introverted attitudes in all types.

FEELING.   The subjective inner valuing process to discern the quality of something i.e. pleasant or unpleasant. The function of consciousness that decides simply whether something is good or bad on an emotional level, i.e. I like/I don't like. Corresponds to Cancer, Scorpio and Pisces in astrology.

INDIVIDUATION.   The process of fulfilment during one lifetime that involves the interplay of positive and negative, yin and yang, dark and light, etc. All life is built on this pair of opposites and an individual attempting to understand his own inner self will have recognized this; both masculine and feminine energies are necessary to one another for growth and maturation on a psychological and physical level. Developing the four functions of consciousness also promotes greater awareness, a balanced outlook and psychological health.

INTROJECTION.   The opposite of projection; becoming conscious of what one has projected on to another, attempting to integrate those contents into one's self thus dissolving the power of the projection. To redirect psychic energy back to the source from where it is created.

INTROVERSION.   The directing of one's energy to the internal, subjective environment, thus continually relying on inner values for stimulus. Nothing impinges upon the introverted type that is not already part of its subjective world.

INTUITION.   The function of the psyche that perceives something unconsciously; the general trend is towards penetration and vision. To intuit something is to grasp its inner meaning, though this happens quite spontaneously. Jung's intuitive types relate best to Aries, Leo and Sagittarius.

IRRATIONAL.   Rational v Irrational in the Jungian sense is the difference between judgement and non-judgement. The thinking/feeling functions are rational since they are to discern the quality and value of something. Sensation and Intuition are non-judgmental since they are to discern the mere existence of something.

LIBIDO.   This is the term used by Jung for psychic energy, although it cannot be measured quantitively like physical energy. It manifests through willing certain states of mind into a particular form, although much will inevitably remain unconscious.

PERSONA.   The outer face of the psyche, the archetype of social adaptation—one's public face that fits hand in glove with the sign on the ascendant, or planets contained in the first house.

PROJECTION.   The releasing of unconscious contents onto an object, almost voluntarily though the subject is unaware of this. The projection is a potential life-form full of psychic energy that finds expression in the object.

PSYCHE.   The mind of man as a whole, living organ, embracing both conscious and unconscious energies. The sum total of man's possible experiences contained in one lifetime, his inner and outer worlds which compensate for each other. The birth chart is an excellent diagram for presenting the psyche.

SELF.   The patterning 'X' factor that somehow gives 'meaning' to one's life. The invisible hand of fate which we invoke by our very own 'free will', the life-path, one's ultimate *raison d'être*. The psyche gravitates towards wholeness with the self at the nucleus. During the course of one lifetime though, it can be seen to be the actual motivation behind the whole psyche itself.

SENSATION.   The function of consciousness that determines the existence of an object via sense impressions. Jung attributes the irrational function to this type, though it is not meant in its usual, everyday sense. The signs Taurus, Virgo and Capricorn are far from irrational, in the sense that we use the word.

SYMBOL.   Almost any experience, situation or object (tangible or otherwise) can be used to symbolize certain human urges, instincts and motivations. The symbol always represents something to a deeper level of meaning which the object could never reach or satisfy by its outer, more obvious meaning.

THINKING.   The function of consciousness that discerns between this and that, telling us what it is and what it is not. It is a relating process, classifying experience according to an objective standpoint, translated as the Air element in astrology, correlated with Gemini, Libra and Aquarius.

UNCONSCIOUS.   A much-bandied-about term and in contrast to Jung's definition of consciousness, must mean that which I do not know and that which I think I do not know. This suggests a state of unawareness, but these factors have the potential to become conscious at any given moment. The unconscious content compensates for the conscious; always balancing the energies assigned to the ego. It can be likened to a great reservoir; full of potential energies waiting to be discovered, released and integrated into the conscious life.

RECOMMENDED READING

Astrology
Relating, Liz Greene, Coventure, 1977.
The Astrology of Fate, Liz Greene, Allen & Unwin, 1984.
Planets in Transit, Robert Hand, Para Research, 1976.
The Pulse of Life, Dane Rudhyar.
The Twelve Houses, Howard Sasportas, Aquarian Press, 1985.
The Lure of the Heavens, Donald Papon, Samuel Weiser, 1972.
Secrets from a Stargazer's Notebook, Debbi Kempton Smith, Bantam Books, 1982.
How to transform your life through Astrology, Robin Macnaughton, Bantam Books, 1983.
Relationships and Life Cycles, Stephen Arroyo, CRCS Publications, 1979.

Depth Psychology
Psychological Types, Carl G. Jung-Coll. Works Vol. 6, Routledge & Kegan Paul, 1971.
The Structure and Dynamics of the Psyche, Carl G. Jung-Coll. Works Vol.8, Routledge & Kegan Paul, 1960.
The Archetypes and the Collective Unconscious, Carl G. Jung-Coll. Works Vol. 9 pt 1, Routledge & Kegan Paul, 1959.
Aion, Carl G. Jung-Coll. Works Vol. 9, pt 11, Routledge & Kegan Paul, 1959.
The I and the not I, M. Esther Harding, Princeton University Press, 1965.
Man and his Symbols, Edited by Carl G. Jung, Aldus Books, 1964.
The Inner World of Childhood, Frances G. Wickes, Coventure.
The Integrity of the Personality, Anthony Storr, Pelican Books, 1963.
A Dictionary of Symbols, Tom Chetwynd, Paladin, 1982.

Philosophy

The Secret of the Golden Flower, Richard Wilhelm and Carl Jung, Routledge & Kegan Paul, 1962.

The First and Last Freedom, J. Krishnamurti, Gollancz, 1954.

Freedom from the Known, J. Krishnamurti, Gollancz, 1969.

The Meaning of Happiness, Alan Watts, Rider, 1978.

The Way of Zen, Alan Watts, Penguin, 1970.

Tao Te Ching, Lao Tzu, Penguin, 1969.

A History of Western Philosophy, Bertrand Russell, Unwin Paperbacks, 1978.

Zen: Direct Pointing to Reality, Anne Bancroft, Thames & Hudson, 1979.

Miscellaneous

Three Magic Words, U. S. Andersen, Wiltshire Book Co., 1954.

Fairy Tales: Allegories of the Inner Life, J. C. Cooper, Aquarian Press, 1983.

Seeing with the Mind's Eye, M. and N. Samuels, Random House, 1976.

Is Christianity True? Michael Arnheim, Duckworth.

A Dictionary for Dreamers, Tom Chetwynd, Granada, 1972.

INDEX